# ECSTASY
# A Way of Knowing

32

# Andrew M. Greeley

is the Director for the Center for the Study of American Pluralism, which is part of the National Opinion Research Center. The author of forty books, Father Greeley—a Catholic priest who holds a doctorate in Sociology from the University of Chicago—also contributes to *New Republic* and *The New York Times*. His most recent books are *New Agenda* and *Sexual Intimacy*.

# ECSTASY
# A Way of Knowing

### ANDREW M. GREELEY

A SPECTRUM BOOK

PRENTICE-HALL, INC., *Englewood Cliffs, New Jersey*

*Library of Congress Cataloging in Publication Data*
GREELEY, ANDREW M.
   Ecstasy; a way of knowing.

   (A Spectrum Book)
   1. Ecstasy.  2. Mysticism.  I. Title.
BL626.G73        301.44        73–22166
ISBN 0–13–234948–5
ISBN 0–13–234930–2 (pbk.)

PRENTICE-HALL INTERNATIONAL, INC. (LONDON)
PRENTICE-HALL OF AUSTRALIA PTY., LTD. (SYDNEY)
PRENTICE-HALL OF CANADA, LTD. (TORONTO)
PRENTICE-HALL OF INDIA PRIVATE LIMITED (NEW DELHI)
PRENTICE-HALL OF JAPAN, INC. (TOKYO)

# Contents

vii

*To William McCready*

*colleague in the study of mysticism—*
*with even better reasons than I have*

# CHAPTER ONE

# A Beginning

It is late at night. A man has driven many miles to a house on the shore of a lake. He parks his car, walks down the steps to a pier jutting out into the water. On this moonless night the man looks up toward the great black umbrella of stars over his head and a feeling of unspeakable peace comes over him. In the next instant of awareness it is morning; he has no idea what happened to all the hours in between.

A young woman has just made love with her husband. They have snatched an interlude together in the middle of the afternoon. It was the best sex they ever had, and she lies exhausted in his arms. Suddenly, a new and very different kind of pleasure takes possession of her. She smiles first and then laughs; her entire body takes on a peculiarly delightful glow. This new pleasure makes intercourse

1

seem mild in comparison. The whole of the universe has somehow flooded her being.

A troubled young man has been listening to Beethoven's Ninth Symphony on a phonograph in his apartment. He turns off the music and begins to work on a term paper, but he makes little progress. The doubts, the fears, the thoughts of self-destruction that have harassed him before return. Then, in counterpoint, he hears the hymn of the Ode to Joy, and something, perhaps someone, takes possession of the room and of him. The doubts, the fears, the anxieties are dispelled forever; the young man *knows* there is nothing to worry about.

A mother bends over her baby's crib. The child is peacefully asleep, and she notices as though for the first time the shape of his tiny ear. It is the greatest work of art she has ever seen. Peace and joy surge through her, and a pale, misty blue light seems to absorb both her and her child for a time that seems both an instant and eternity.

Something dramatic has occurred in each of these four cases to alter the consciousness of the people involved; and it is something that has happened in all times and in all places of the human condition as we know it. The four people have experienced an interlude of mystical ecstasy. What has really happened? Was it only a brief schizophrenic episode? Have they regressed to child-like behavior? Are they reflecting on their own thought processes? Are they mad? Have they infused some foreign chemical into their bloodstreams?

Or have they awakened, leaving us in our lives still asleep? Is it possible that God has come down upon them, and that the Holy Spirit has taken possession of their souls? Are they lunatics or saints? Are they retreating from the real world or only beginning to discover it? Should we seek what has happened to them or do our best to avoid it? Perhaps we have only to wait patiently and hope that it will happen to us too.

Until very recently social science research would have subsumed the mystical experience under the rubric "abnormal behavior," which includes all other states of altered consciousness. In a rationalized, formalized, bureaucratized, scientific, technological world the mystic was a deviant, an abnormal, a misfit. Even today, most of the research done by social scientists to explain mysticism is really an effort to explain it away. Ecstasy, we are told in effect, is like some other forms of deviant behavior that we already understand (schizophrenia or regression in particular). Thus there is nothing mysterious about it, and there is no need for it to trouble us (though the implication that it does trouble us is usually not explicitly recognized). Some of the more recent research, however, has been rather sympathetic to ecstatic experience. One wing of the psychological profession, deeply influenced by a study of Oriental religion and drug-induced altered states of consciousness, is willing to treat the ecstatic with some interest and respect. Most enthusiastic members of this wing (in particular if they are associated with Esalen) will even suggest that the ecstatic has discovered a new dimension of human consciousness that the rest of us can learn to develop and that will make the world a more peaceful and human place in the process.

Psychological misfit or prophet of the New Age, incipient schizophrenic or counterculture folk hero, the ecstatic can choose whichever role he wants. But the four people described in the beginning of the chapter are not misfits or schizophrenics; they are, on the contrary, healthy, normally functioning human beings who differ from others only in that they seem more happy than the average person one encounters in daily life. They are not part of the counterculture; the strongest drugs any of them take are an aspirin for headache and an occasional Scotch and water before dinner (and in one case, a Stinger or two afterwards). Only one of them would use the word "mystical" to describe his experience, and another will say quite frankly that she thought everybody had experiences like hers. They do not hypnotize themselves into trances, they do not spend time in Zen or Yoga meditations, they don't repeat mysterious formulae over and over to themselves, and they probably wouldn't go near Esalen if their lives depended on it.

Nor are they particularly abnormal even in the statistical sense. There is an increasing amount of research evidence to show that experiences like theirs are not infrequent. If social science has believed that the ecstatic experience is rare in the United States (it accepts anthropological revelations of its being commonplace in more exotic and more interesting places), the reason may be that few if any social scientists would know an ecstatic experience if it were labeled in neon.

William McCready and I are doing research that suggests that an occasional mystical experience (sometimes very intense) is not at all uncommon. There are perhaps millions of people in our society who have such experiences with some frequency. The fact that social science is uninterested in them does not seem to have bothered these people at all—probably because most of them have never read any social science literature on the ecstatic phenomenon.

Most social scientists are unwilling to take mystics at their own words. The psychotherapist says the ecstatic has experienced something "rather like schizophrenia"; the Esalen psychologist says the mystic has been through a "feeling state of heightened consciousness." Such categorizing doubtless helps researchers to organize their work; however, in doing so they are paying little heed to what the mystic says happened. According to *him,* the experience is more one of *knowing* than of feeling. If anything is heightened in the ecstatic interlude, it is the cognitive faculties of the mystic: he knows something others do not know and that he did not know before. He *sees,* he *understands,* he *perceives,* he *comprehends.* The occasional mystic who has pursued the psychological and psychiatric literature becomes impatient with the insensitivity of the writers: "They really haven't been listening," is the most common criticism. They don't realize that, above all, the mystic *knows* that cognition is at the core of his experience.

In the work that McCready and I are doing we are trying to take the mystics at their words. We are assuming that ecstasy is basically a cognitive phenomenon, that the mystic is describing precisely what happens when he says that for the first time he "sees things the way they really are." As social scientists we are not prepared to say that what the mystic sees is indeed the way things really are, though we must admit that there is both a confidence and authenticity about their descriptions that is persuasive. But we do insist that mystics are not freaks in either the old sense of the word or in the more recent counterculture sense.

In this book I wish to provide a preliminary perspective for the study and understanding of the ecstatic experience, a perspective on both the assumption that the mystic must be taken at his own word when he says that his experience is one of heightened cognition and also on the traditional wisdom of my religion, which has always respected mystics while asserting that mysticism is not the ultimate in religious behavior. Against the old psychotherapeutic approach—which is still quite common in social science—I shall contend that the mystics are not lunatics; and against the new faddism, I insist that there is something to religion beyond mysticism, namely, loving service.

In addition, I wish to draw as sharp a line as I can between mysticism and the "mystical," by which is frequently meant the occult. There are many different kinds of altered states of consciousness, and in the course of this book I shall make use of one explanatory model on which to build my own theory of what happens during a mystical interlude. Undoubtedly, many of those who are now interested in mysticism are also interested in the occult. They are quite incapable of differentiating between John of the Cross and Anton Szandor La Vey, although each holds out the attraction of being very different from the square society in which the occultists were raised and to which they will most probably return. But while both the witch and the mystic experience altered states of consciousness, and while novelty-hungry children of the rich might be interested in both as a way of rebelling against their parents, the two are very different. The powers the mystic deals with are totally different from those the witch claims to be in touch with, and the experiences of the mystical and the occult are categorically different.

The four people I described at the beginning of this chapter are not witches, they are not "into" the occult, they are not rebelling against a square society, they are not running away from anything. Mysticism and ecstasy existed in the human condition even in the Western world and even in technological America well before Timothy Leary, LSD, and Esalen. But Esalen and Timothy Leary may be only the tip of the iceberg. There are a number of important cultural changes going on that will permit the considerable number of mystics we have in our population to talk more freely about their experiences. These changes, and I shall discuss them later in the book, may also allow the mystics among us to respond to such experiences with less uncertainty and anxiety. Others of us may feel free to develop mystical tendencies we have previously repressed. I do not know whether my book or any like it can be of much use to the authentic ecstatic. What, after all, do I have to tell him? He understands far better than I do. But it is possible that there are large numbers of others who experience occasional twinges of ecstasy and are afraid of them because they do not want to become "freaks" in either sense of the word. It is for those people that this book is primarily intended.

Charles Meyer has recently pointed out to me that humankind may well be on a pilgrimage from Antioch to Alexandria, from the mystadelic to the mystagogic, from trying to explain all mystery and all problems to being content with the exploration of mystery. Until very recently we were convinced that science could explain everything, that there was nothing mysterious left in the universe. If we didn't understand everything ourselves, some scientist somewhere did, or if he did not someone soon would.

When I was a graduate student in the early 1960s, this serene confidence in the explanatory power of science would not have been questioned, I think, by either my fellow students or my teachers. Within a decade, however, there has been a dramatic change. We are conscious even within the scientific enterprise itself that every answer generates new, more complex and difficult questions. But we also understand now that science cannot explain everything. The great mysteries—why is there anything at all, and why is there the titanic struggle between good and evil in the universe, the human race, and in each of us?—can never be explained anyway. Those mysteries can never be resolved.

And so we seek now not explanations or answers but interpretations. We are interested in symbols that will illumine the darkness cast by mystery, rather than formulae to sweep the mystery away. We want to plumb the depths of the mystery so that we can understand better. We no longer want or expect to understand everything. The universe becomes sacred again precisely because it is mysterious. It is now once again able to surprise us.

In this changing climate where mystery is once more respected and where we are looking for illumination rather than explanation, mystical ecstasy becomes much more important for two reasons. First of all, the ecstatic claims to have seen things the way they really are, to have penetrated to the absolute depths of mystery. His testimony about the way things really are in a mystagogic world is at least as important as the testimony of the scientist. We are not yet prepared to take our ecstatics as seriously as we take our nuclear physicists, our microbiologists, or even our survey research sociologists, although there have been eras in human history when the mystic was taken more seriously than the scientist. However, the logic in our new conviction that the universe is an open one after all means that we must listen attentively to what the mystic has to say. Scientists may be conceded their own particular form of cognition, but then, at least in a mystagogic world, one must also concede to mystics the legitimacy of the form of cognition they claim to have. If the scientist has the right to sit in judgment of the mystic, it may also be the case that the mystic has the right to sit in judgment of the scientist. Perhaps the two can fruitfully listen to each other. Indeed, as a social scientist, I am engaged precisely in the effort of trying to listen seriously to what the mystics tell me.

Secondly, not only is the mystic a potential interpreter of the "other world," of the supermundane, even of the transcendental, he also confirms that there is something (others might say Someone) out there. If mystics are not complete madmen, if they are not raving lunatics, then there are other dimensions to life than our commonplace, commonsense, everyday technological world view would be willing to concede. The mystic, by virtue of his encounter with a realm very different from that most of us experience, stands as a sign that the universe is indeed mysterious—far more mysterious than it appeared to me at the University of Chicago in 1961.

There are many layers of the human mind, many levels of human knowing. Our cognition is not the one-dimensional activity that B. F. Skinner would attempt to sell us, nor is it the three-dimensional activity of the Freudians. There are strange and baffling things which the human mind is capable of encompassing. That we wish to understand these little-known forms of knowledge better does not mean we think to understand them merely by categorizing them, or that we assume that they can ever be understood fully. It does mean that we will try to learn more about them by exploring the possibility that in these mysterious forms of knowledge we may penetrate more deeply into the great mysteries of the universe.

Those who have been through a mystical experience tell us that there is nothing in the world quite like it. In his classic work, *The Varieties of Religious Experience,* William James recounts an experience of James Russell Lowell:

"I had a revelation last Friday evening [Lowell reported]. I was at Mary's, and happening to say something of the presence of spirits (of whom, I said, I was often dimly aware), Mr. Putnam entered into an argument with me on spiritual matters. As I was speaking, the whole system rose up before me like a vague destiny looming from the Abyss. I never before so clearly felt the Spirit of God in me and around me. The whole room seemed to me full of God. The air seemed to waver to and fro with the presence of Something I knew not what. I spoke with the calmness and clearness of a prophet. I cannot tell you what this revelation was. I have not yet studied it enough. But I shall perfect it one day, and then you shall hear it and acknowledge its grandeur. . . ." [1]

He then turns to two even more detailed descriptions of similar events. The first concerns the experience of a clergyman:

"I remember the night, and almost the very spot on the hilltop, where my soul opened out, as it were, into the Infinite, and there was a rushing together of two worlds, the inner and the outer. It was deep calling unto deep,—the deep that my own struggle had opened up within being answered by the unfathomable deep without, reaching beyond the stars. I stood alone with Him who had made me, and all the beauty of the world, and love, and sorrow, and even temptation. I did not see Him, but felt the perfect unison of my spirit with His. The ordinary sense of things around me faded. For the moment nothing but an ineffable joy and exaltation remained. It is impossible fully to describe the experience. It was like the effect of some great orchestra when all the separate notes have melted into

[1] William James, *The Varieties of Religious Experience.* New York: The New American Library, a Mentor Book, 1958, p. 67.

one swelling harmony that leaves the listener conscious of nothing save that his soul is being wafted upwards, and almost bursting with its own emotion. The perfect stillness of the night was thrilled by a more solemn silence. The darkness held a presence that was all the more felt because it was not seen. I could not any more have doubted that *He* was there than that I was. Indeed, I felt myself to be, if possible, the less real of the two.

"My highest faith in God and truest idea of him were then born in me. I have stood upon the Mount of Vision since, and felt the Eternal round about me. But never since has there come quite the same stirring of the heart. Then, if ever, I believe, I stood face to face with God, and was born anew of his spirit. There was, as I recall it, no sudden change of thought or belief, except that my early crude conception had, as it were, burst into flower. There was no destruction of the old, but a rapid, wonderful unfolding. Since that time no discussion that I have heard of the proofs of God's existence has been able to shake my faith. Having once felt the presence of God's spirit, I have never lost it again for long. My most assuring evidence of his existence is deeply rooted in that hour of vision, in the memory of that supreme experience, and in the conviction, gained from reading and reflection, that something the same has come to all who have found God. I am aware that it may justly be called mystical. I am not enough acquainted with philosophy to defend it from that or any other charge. I feel that in writing of it I have overlaid it with words rather than put it clearly to your thought. But, such as it is, I have described it as carefully as I now am able to do." [2]

James translated this account from the original French and written by a Swiss:

"I was in perfect health: we were on our sixth day of tramping, and in good training. We had come the day before from Sixt to Trient by Buet. I felt neither fatigue, hunger, nor thirst, and my state of mind was equally healthy. I had had at Forlaz good news from home; I was subject to no anxiety, either near or remote, for we had a good guide, and there was not a shadow of uncertainty about the road we should follow. I can best describe the condition in which I was by calling it a state of equilibrium. When all at once I experienced a feeling of being raised above myself, I felt the presence of God—I tell of the thing just as I was conscious of it—as if his goodness and his power were penetrating me altogether. The throb of

[2] *Ibid.*, pp. 67–68.

emotion was so violent that I could barely tell the boys to pass on and not wait for me. I then sat down on a stone, unable to stand any longer, and my eyes overflowed with tears. I thanked God that in the course of my life he had taught me to know him, that he sustained my life and took pity both on the insignificant creature and on the sinner that I was. I begged him ardently that my life might be consecrated to the doing of his will. I felt his reply, which was that I should do his will from day to day, in humility and poverty, leaving him, the Almighty God, to be judge of whether I should some time be called to bear witness, more conspicuously. Then, slowly, the ecstasy left my heart; that is, I felt that God had withdrawn the communion which he had granted, and I was able to walk on, but very slowly, so strongly was I still possessed by the interior emotion. Besides, I had wept uninterruptedly for several minutes, my eyes were swollen, and I did not wish my companions to see me. The state of ecstasy may have lasted four or five minutes, although it seemed at the time to last much longer. My comrades waited for me ten minutes at the cross of Barine, but I took about twenty-five or thirty minutes to join them, for as well as I can remember, they said that I had kept them back for about half an hour. The impression had been so profound that in climbing slowly the slope I asked myself if it were possible that Moses on Sinai could have had a more intimate communication with God. I think it well to add that in this ecstasy of mine, God had neither form, color, odor, nor taste; moreover, that the feeling of his presence was accompanied with no determinate localization. It was rather as if my personality had been transformed by the presence of a *spiritual spirit*. But the more I seek words to express this intimate intercourse, the more I feel the impossibility of describing the thing by any of our usual images. At bottom the expression most apt to render what I felt is this: God was present, though invisible; he fell under no one of my sense, yet my consciousness perceived him." [3]

These are obviously spectacular events. Most of us would be inclined to believe that these kinds of intense experience happened only in the past or only in primitive regions today. If Professor Rudolf Bultmann was right when he said that a man who could control the powers of electricity with a flick of a switch no longer needed religious myths, it would seem *a fortiori* that humankind, with atomic energy at its command, hardly needs such flights of ecstatic fancy as those we have quoted. As recently as a decade ago

[3] *Ibid.*, pp. 68–69.

a mystical experience would probably have been treated by most intelligent people who heard about it as a form of mental illness, perhaps a mild bout of schizophrenia. There were, of course, little groups around the country, some of them even scholarly, who took mysticism—usually of the Oriental variety—very seriously. But it was an era when Harvey Cox was celebrating the glory of the "Secular City" and Daniel Callahan was announcing to his readers that "many Catholics" (by which he meant himself and his friends) no longer needed the liturgy. If there were any mystics in the Catholic Church, they kept it a deep, dark secret, because clearly a mystic would not be a very effective second-grade teacher or assistant pastor.

All that has changed, of course, and now mysticism is very fashionable again—perhaps dangerously so. Yet there is every reason to believe that the experience of mystical union may well be a relatively constant phenomenon. Whether such experiences are noticed or not is probably a function of whether they are at any given moment culturally acceptable. Abraham Maslow has suggested that almost everyone he studied had some sort of "peak-experience," by which he meant an intense feeling of unity with the universe and of one's own place within that unity. Marghanita Laski,[4] in her pioneering study (based on a nonrepresentative sample), found that "sensations of transcendent ecstasy" were widespread. Professor Morton Lieberman of the Committee of Human Development, University of Chicago, studied students in California and reported that half of his respondents had had some kind of mystical experience, although half of that half reported their experiences had occurred under the influence of drugs. In research that McCready and I are doing (mentioned earlier in this chapter) there is evidence that one-half of the American population would report having experiences of union with "a powerful spiritual force that draws me out of myself." About one-fifth would report frequent such experiences. We may conclude tentatively at least that the capacity for transient episodes of ecstasy is widespread in the population. Whether many people have experiences as intense as those described previously must remain prob-

[4] Marghanita Laski, *Ecstasy: A Study of Some Secular and Religious Experiences.* Westport, Connecticut: Greenwood Press, 1968. Reprinted from the 1962 edition.

lematic, though it is at least arguable that a considerable number of people may well have them but do not bother to write them down or are reluctant to do so.

I was discussing this book with a young married couple, and the woman asked me what I meant by "mystical experience." I told her that it was something like Maslow's peak-experience, that is, a feeling of intense unity with the universe and of one's place within that unity. She looked surprised, "But doesn't everybody have those kinds of experiences?" she asked.

Her husband and I admitted that we didn't. "But I have them all the time," she said. Further questioning revealed that her frequent experiences were of the sort that one can find in any book on ecstasy, and that indeed on several occasions she had even experienced the pale blue light that marks the most powerful of them. The young woman was a bona fide mystic without even realizing it. She never thought her experiences worth reporting to her husband, who was as astonished as I to hear of them.

This book will focus on the ecstatic interlude of the sort typified by the four vignettes that began this chapter and by those excerpted from William James. I do not equate mysticism with haunted houses, Oiuja boards, spiritualism, astrology, witchcraft, diabolism, Druidism, the White Legion, or the Church of the Process. These and similar phenomena are occurring at the same time and among some of the same people who are also hunting for ecstasy, and they are in substantial part the result of the same cultural and historical phenomena that have led to a reawakening of interest in mysticism. But to confuse the occult with the mystical is to define the field so broadly that it becomes incapable of analysis; it is also to mix the kooky and the crazy with the sublime and the profound.[5]

Pentecostalism will also not be dealt with in this book. While the Pentecostal movement seems to represent the same hunger for religious experience as the renewed interest in mysticism, it does not represent the mystical or the ecstatic experience as these words have traditionally been understood. The tongue-speaking phenomenon of

[5] For a book that does lump ecstasy together with all matter of weird and bizarre behavior and movements, see Richard Woods, *The Occult Revolution: Christian Meditation*. New York: Herder & Herder, 1971.

Pentecostalism certainly does represent a form of behavior in which mind exercises unusual control over bodily functions, but it is not ecstasy in the traditional sense of the word.

Nor am I especially concerned with such phenomena as biofeedback, whereby brain researchers have been able to train humans to obtain visceral control of bodily processes such as blood pressure, heartbeat, and brain waves, or the trance-induced learning experiences developed by Jean Houston and her colleagues, who first used LSD and now use "trance machines." These areas of research are extremely important and may very well deal with human capabilities that are closely related to if not quite the same as the capability for mystical union, but research is not yet far enough advanced for one to say with confidence that mysticism and biofeedback are really the same thing. In any case, we should clarify our thoughts about what the mystical experience is, in the strict sense of the word, before we can decide whether it is the same as or similar to these other phenomena.

ESP, telekinesis, clairvoyance, and the related psychic phenomena studied by Dr. Rhine and his colleagues and disciples will not play a large part in this volume either. I take the evidence in favor of ESP and similar phenomena very seriously. Like visceral control and trance-induced learning, it appears to represent an expansion of human consciousness; but for the moment I am not willing to assume that it is the same sort of expanded consciousness that occurs in a moment of mystical ecstasy. (Dr. McCready and I, however, are also studying the prevalence of ESP-like experiences in our national sample.)

On the other hand, in this book drug-induced ecstasy is not excluded from consideration. I am profoundly suspicious of such experiences, and while I am not sure that R. C. Zehner[6] is correct when he argues that drug-induced ecstasy is completely different from religious ecstasy, I am still ill at ease when someone suggests to me that John of the Cross's ascent of Mt. Carmel is really the same thing the experience of an acid-head hippie in an attic in Berkeley. However, I see no reason to deny that drugs can trigger the operation of a person's capacities for the ecstatic.

6 *Mysticism: Sacred and Profane.* New York: Oxford University Press, 1957.

We will be concerned here with mysticism in a strict sense, whether it be Eastern or Western, drug-induced or "natural," intense or mild, frequent or occasional. I am not speaking of all forms of consciousness-expansion, nor am I concerned with all the bizarre things one can read about in the books on the occult rack of paperback bookstores.[7]

My purpose in writing this book is to present a pragmatic, skeptical, hard-nosed analysis of both the mystical experience and the mystical revival. As will be seen in subsequent pages, I believe that the capacity for ecstasy is part of the human condition, that no special supernatural intervention need be postulated, and that the current craze about "expanded consciousness" must be viewed with considerable reserve. Nevertheless, in the midst of all the kookiness that marks the so-called occult revolution, there is in the current revival of mysticism a sign of the times that no one can afford to ignore.

[7] See Arnold Ludwig, "Altered States of Consciousness," in Raymond Prince (ed.), *Trance and Possession States*, Montreal: R. M. Bucke Memorial Society, 1968. In this fascinating article Ludwig lists sixty-three forms of "altered states of consciousness." They are reproduced in Appendix B to this volume; I am dealing mainly with state D-1. In Ludwig's bibliography, there are ninety-six references listed—enough to keep anyone busy who wishes to explore the whole question of altered consciousness.

# CHAPTER TWO

# What Is the Mystical Experience?

Louis Armstrong is alleged to have remarked once that rhythm is "what if you've got it, you don't need a definition; and if you don't got it, no definition is any good." The readers of this book who have had encounters with the transcendent will find my description of it most inadequate. Most, like myself, whose moments of ecstasy are so brief as to be almost nonexistent, will only dimly understand what the process is like; yet one must try to describe it, if only to distinguish a mystical experience from other phenomena. Our best guide to a description of mysticism is still William James.

James sees four characteristics which mark such experiences:[1]

1. *Ineffability.* Mystical union is something that defies expression. It is a state of feeling that must be directly experienced and

[1] James, *op. cit.*, pp. 292–93.

cannot be transferred or imparted to others. In James' words, "One must have musical ears to know the value of a symphony; one must have been in love oneself to understand a lover's state of mind. Lacking the heart or ear, we cannot interpret the musician or the lover justly, and are even likely to consider him weak-minded or absurd. The mystic finds that most of us accord to his experiences an equally incompetent treatment." [2]

2. *Noetic quality.* The mystic has an overwhelming experience of understanding. He sees things with a fantastic clarity. (This is a point that is reported very often in experiences of drug-induced ecstasy.) Maslow tells us that in the "peak-experiences" he studied, the person involved sees the unity of the universe and his own integration with it. One need only read Teilhard de Chardin's *Letters from a Traveller* to realize that he was a mystic whose entire world view, so brilliantly expressed in many books, was simply an attempt to explicate a profound mystical insight. In James' words, "Mystical experiences are states of insight into depths of truth unplumbed by the discursive intellect. They are illuminations, revelations, full of significance and importance, all inarticulate thought they remain; and as a rule they carry with them a curious sense of authority for after-time." [3]

3. *Transiency.* The mystical experience is transient. In her empirical research Marghanita Laski reports that the ecstatic interlude was very bried indeed—a few moments, a half-hour at the most—though there was an added time of "coming back down to earth" after the episode. James comments: "Mystical states cannot be sustained for long. Except in rare instances, half an hour, or at most an hour or two, seems to be the limit beyond which they fade into the light of common day." [4] I suspect that he includes in his definition not only the moments of ecstasy themselves but that which Laski calls "the afterglow." When one's experience has "faded into the light of common day," then even the aftereffects have pretty well vanished, and it may be difficult to even remember what the experience was like. As James says, "Often, when faded, their quality can

2 *Ibid.*, p. 293.
3 *Ibid.*, p. 293.
4 *Ibid.*, p. 293.

but imperfectly be reproduced in memory; but when they recur it is recognized; and from one recurrence to another it is susceptible of continuous development in what is felt as inner richness and importance." [5] There is, then, some kind of continuity between such experiences, though when one is not immediately involved in the experience, the thread of continuity seems lost; in fact, it is there, though unrecognized.

4. *Passivity*. There may be all sorts of things one can do to induce a mystical experience—pray, meditate, undergo hypnosis, listen to music, take a drug, impose intense discipline on the senses —but these are all by way of preparation; they merely put one in a state in which something else seems to happen, another power seems to take over. As James observes: "Although the oncoming of mystical states may be facilitated by preliminary voluntary operations, as by fixing the attention, or going through certain bodily performances, or in other ways which manuals of mysticism prescribe; yet when the characteristic sort of consciousness once has set in, the mystic feels as if his own will were in abeyance, and indeed sometimes as if he were grasped and held by a superior power." [6] Something besides the conscious, self-controlling reality principle is operating. According to the great mystics of the Christian tradition, God himself intervenes. But while I believe that in a certain sense such an assertion might be the truth, one need not postulate some special divine intervention. In fact, what is happening is that deep powers in the human personality, normally latent, take over and produce in us experiences of knowledge and insight that are simply not available in daily life. But more of that in a later chapter.

In another mysticism classic, written in 1901, Richard M. Bucke, himself, unlike James, a mystic, describes a "cosmic consciousness" that is similar to the paradigm of James:

1. "The person, suddenly, without warning, has a sense of being immersed in a flame, or rose-colored cloud, or perhaps rather a sense that the mind is itself filled with such a cloud of haze." [7] (This

5 *Ibid.,* p. 193.
6 *Ibid.,* p. 193.
7 Richard M. Bucke, "From Self to Cosmic Consciousness," in John White (ed.), *The Highest State of Consciousness.* Garden City, N.Y.: Doubleday, Anchor Books, 1972, p. 86.

experience of light, though not reported by all mystics, seems to be widespread. Indeed, as Mircea Eliade notes, it is to be found in almost all other cultures. So, too, is the sense of being "caught in flame." See, for example, Richard Rolle, *The Fire of Love,* Penguin edition, 1972.)

2. The ecstatic is possessed by joy, for he perceives that all things are well. As Bucke puts it, ". . . he is, as it were, bathed in an emotion of joy, assurance, triumph, 'salvation.' The last word is not strictly correct if taken in its ordinary sense, for the feeling, when fully developed, is not that a particular act of salvation is affected, but that no special 'salvation' is needed, the scheme upon which the world is built, being itself sufficient." [8]

3. Bucke also records, as does James, an experience of intellectual illumination: "Like a flash there is presented . . . a clear conception (a vision) in outline of the meaning and drift of the universe. He does not come to believe merely; but he sees and knows that the cosmos, which to the Self-Conscious mind seems to be made up of dead matter, is in fact far otherwise—is in very truth a living presence." [9] Bucke adds later, "He sees that the life which is in man is eternal, as all life is eternal; that the soul of man is as immortal as God is; that the universe is so built and ordered that without any peradventure all things work together for the good of each and all; that the foundation principle of the world is what we call love, and that the happiness of every individual is in the long run absolutely certain." [10]

Bucke wrote from within the Christian religious tradition. Mystics almost universally report an "illumination" as part of their experience, but it is usually an illumination within the context of the world view to which they are committed (or which they have absorbed through their culture). As Marghanita Laski's research makes clear, not all mystics are religious men and women, and for many of them the illumination is not necessarily a confirmation of the benignity or graciousness of the universe. Some mystical experiences,

[8] Bucke in White, *op. cit.,* p. 87.
[9] *Ibid.,* p. 87.
[10] *Ibid.,* p. 87.

especially those that are drug-induced, lead to a very pessimistic or even despairing world view.

Bucke also contends that in the moment of Cosmic Consciousness there comes "a sense of immortality," an "elimination of the fear of death" and "the sense of sin," and, finally, even adds "charm to the personality" and a change in the appearance that may "amount to a veritable 'transfiguration.' " [11] All of this, he argues, occurs because the mystic knows without learning and from the mere fact of his illumination "(1) that the universe is not a dead machine but a living presence; (2) that in its essence and tendency it is infinitely good; (3) that individual existence is continuous beyond what is called death." [12]

An Oriental mystic might choose to use different belief systems to explicate what happens in a mystical interlude. Thus, instead of describing life beyond death, he might choose to stress the integration of the self into some higher, more immutable reality. But there can be little doubt that both Bucke and the Oriental would be discussing what would be fundamentally the same kind of experience.

Of all the contemporary psychologists who have addressed themselves to mystical phenomena, Abraham Maslow is the most sympathetic and the most perceptive, and his book *Religions, Values, and Peak-Experiences* (Ohio State University Press, 1964) ought to be read by those interested in the mystical phenomena. The most characteristic quality of the peak-experience, according to Maslow, is that the universe is "perceived as an integrated and unified whole." This experience is not merely verbal or intellectual but pervades the being and is "so profound and shaking . . . that it can change the person's character . . . forever after." [13] When one perceives that the universe is a unified whole and that one has a place in it, one can overcome extreme mental stresses, and Maslow reports that one of his patients was permanently cured of chronic anxiety neurosis and another of obsessional thoughts of suicide.

11 *Ibid.*, pp. 88–89.
12 *Ibid.*, p. 90.
13 Abraham Maslow, "The 'Core-Religious' or 'Transcendent' Experience," in White, *op. cit.*, p. 357.

During the peak-experience, a kind of knowledge occurs that Maslow calls "B-cognition":

In the peak-experiences, we become more detached, more objective, and are more able to perceive the world as if it were independent not only of the perceiver but even of human beings in general. The perceiver can more readily look upon nature as if it were there in itself and for itself, not simply as if it were a human playground put there for human purposes. He can more easily refrain from projecting human purposes upon it. In a word, he can see it in its own Being (as an end in itself) rather than as something to be used or something to be afraid of or something to wish for or to be reacted to in some other personal, human, self-centered way.[14]

The person who has a peak-experience can be, at least temporarily, "self-forgetful, egoless, unselfish." He experiences a moment in which he is validated and self-justified. Despite the disorientation of time and space, he sees the world as beautiful, good, desirable, worthwhile, and is even able to accept and understand evil itself as having a proper place in the world. Maslow argues that the peak-experience is always a beautiful one, though he admits that his methods of research might reveal only raptures, failing to uncover experiences of pessimism and despair, which surely are part of drug-induced ecstasies and may also occur in "intellectual" ecstasies.

Maslow's peak-experiences are eminently positive:

In the peak-experience, such emotions as wonder, awe, reverence, humility, surrender, and even worship before the greatness of the experience are often reported. This may go so far as to involve thoughts of death in a peculiar way. Peak-experiences can be so wonderful that they can parallel the experience of dying, that is of an eager and happy dying. It is a kind of reconciliation and acceptance of death. Scientists have never considered as a scientific problem the question of the "good death"; but here in these experiences, we discover a parallel to what has been considered to be the religious attitude toward death, i.e., humility or dignity before it, willingness to accept it, possibly even a happiness with it.[15]

Maslow goes on to say that in "peak-experiences, the dichotomies, polarities, and conflicts of life are transcended or resolved." [16]

14 *Ibid.*, p. 359.
15 *Ibid.*, p. 362.
16 *Ibid.*, p. 362.

There is a loss, though transient, of fear, anxiety, inhibition, of defense and control, of perplexity, confusion, conflict, of delay and restraint. The profound fear of disintegration, of insanity, of death, all tend to disappear for the moment." [17] For Maslow, the peak-experience is "a visit to a personally defined heaven from which the person then returns to earth." [18] Upon his return, the person "feels himself more than at other times to be responsible, active, the creative center of his own activities and of his own perceptions, more self-determined, more a free agent, with more 'free will' than at other times." [19]

TABLE 1. Percentages of the total number of people (112) reporting certain feelings

| FEELINGS | NUMBER OF PEOPLE | PER CENT |
|---|---|---|
| New world/life, satisfaction, joy, salvation, glory | 82 | 73 |
| Knowledge by identification | 76 | 68 |
| New and/or mystical knowledge | 61 | 54 |
| Intensity | 59 | 53 |
| Loss of words/images, sense | 57 | 51 |
| Unity, eternity, heaven | 56 | 50 |
| Up-feelings | 56 | 50 |
| Contact | 48 | 43 |
| Loss of worldliness, desire, sorrow, sin | 42 | 38 |
| Enlargement, improvement | 41 | 37 |
| Loss of self | 40 | 36 |
| Inside-feelings | 38 | 34 |
| Loss of difference, time, place | 29 | 26 |
| Light/fire | 28 | 25 |
| Peace, calm | 27 | 24 |
| Liquidity | 26 | 23 |
| Ineffability | 24 | 21 |
| Release | 18 | 16 |
| Pain | 18 | 16 |
| Withdrawal | 10 | 9 |
| Dark-feelings | 4 | 4 |
| Loss of limitation | 3 | 3 |

17 *Ibid.*, p. 362.
18 *Ibid.*, p. 363.
19 *Ibid.*, p. 363.

He is more loving, more accepting, more spontaneous, more honest, more innocent, less an object, less a "thing," less striving, less selfish, more giving. He has had a glimpse of the way things are and has been transformed by it.

Marghanita Laski presents a table showing the number and percent of her respondents who report various feelings as a result of their moments of "transcendent ecstasy." [20]

We can see that the Laski research, unsystematic as it is, confirms the descriptions of Maslow, Bucke, and James.

Finally, Laski also presents a fascinating table of the percentage distribution of "trigger," [21] the preconditions that apparently bring an ecstatic interlude into being:

TABLE 2.

| TRIGGERS | NONBELIEVERS | | CHRISTIANS | |
|---|---|---|---|---|
| | NO. | % | NO. | % |
| 1. Nature | 16 | 20.2 | 6 | 15.0 |
| 2. Sexual love | 17 | 21.5 | 3 | 7.5 |
| 3. Childbirth | 4 | 5.1 | — | — |
| 4. Exercise, movement | 6 | 7.6 | 1 | 2.5 |
| 5. Religion | 4 | 5.1 | 7 | 17.5 |
| 6. Art | 14 | 17.7 | 12 | 30.0 |
| 7. a. Scientific knowledge | 5 | 6.3 | — | — |
|     b. Poetic knowledge | 1 | 1.3 | 1 | 2.5 |
| 8. Creative work | 4 | 5.1 | 3 | 7.5 |
| 9. Recollection, introspection | 2 | 2.5 | — | — |
| 10. "Beauty" | 2 | 2.5 | 3 | 7.5 |
| 11. Miscellaneous | 4 | 5.1 | 4 | 10.0 |
| TOTAL | 79 | 100.0 | 40 | 100.0 |

There are a number of striking phenomena about this table. More than half of the triggers for Christians derive from nature, religion, and art, while two-fifths of the triggers reported by non-believers have to do with nature and sexual love. Laski suggests that the absence of sexual love as a trigger among Christians may be the

[20] Marghanita Laski, *Ecstasy*. Bloomington, Ind.: University of Indiana Press, 1961, pp. 488–89.
[21] *Ibid.*, p. 494.

result of the fact that the Christian mystical tradition has been a celibate one, and Christians have not believed it possible that sexual intercourse could produce profound religious experience; hence, for them it has not done so. Incidentally, Laski also notes that those whose experiences have been triggered by lovemaking report that it is quite different and decisively distinct from the lovemaking which produced it.[22]

In the traditional Christian perspective, there is a description of mysticism that is not at all out of harmony with those described by the authors we have already quoted. The Anglican dom David Knowles, in his *English Mystical Tradition,* says there are three ways that we may know God: by the natural process of reasoning and natural theology, by revelation—God's own self-disclosure through scriptures—and by the mystical form of knowledge. His description of the last follows:

. . . there is a third by which God and the truths of Christianity can not only be believed and acted upon, but can in varying degrees be directly known and experienced. . . . This knowledge, this experience, which is never entirely separable from an equally immediate and experimental union with God by love, has three main characteristics. It is recognized by the person concerned as something utterly different from and more real and adequate than all his previous knowledge and love of God. It is experienced as something at once immanent and received, something moving and filling the powers of mind and soul. It is felt as taking place at a deeper level of the personality and soul than that on which the normal processes of thought and will take place, and the mystic is aware, both in himself and in others, of the soul, its qualities and of the divine presence and action within it, as something wholly distinct from the reasoning mind with its powers. Finally, this experience is wholly incommunicable, save as a bare statement, and in this respect all the utterances of the mystics are entirely inadequate as representations of the mystical experience, but it brings absolute cer-

---

22 Laski suggests that the lack of childbirth triggers among Christians may be due to there being fewer married women among her Christian respondents. This might also have a bearing on the lack of lovemaking triggers among her Christian respondents.

It is worth noting that in preliminary research done for the National Opinion Research Center on a Catholic population only, sexual love was not mentioned; however, childbirth was mentioned frequently as a trigger.

tainty to the mind of the recipient. This is the traditional mystical theology, the knowledge of God, in its purest form.[23]

In summary, then, there seems to be an evident convergence among the various attempts to describe the mystical experience. It is a breaking away from everyday life and an instantaneous, fantastically powerful emersion into a transformed unity which illuminates the person, exalts him, and transforms him, at least temporarily. He sees things *the way they are* and finds himself in the possession of a power much greater than he, which overwhelms him with joy.

Furthermore, the process is in a sense unexpected, regardless of whether it has been arduously sought or not. Whatever it is, something powerful takes control of the personality. Even if one has induced the experience by ingesting chemicals, the experience nonetheless seems quite independent of the inducing agent, which has only released the barriers that stand in the way of the operation of this tremendous force. The sunset may be like any other sunset, but at this particular time and place something else happens. The elimination of distractions, which may be effected by a long exercise of Yoga discipline, may have been achieved as on any other day; but on this particular day something unique and special occurs. An interlude of lovemaking may have been no more pleasurable than last night's; but on this occasion something special occurs that is quite distinct from it and before which orgasm lacks intensity. Small wonder that ecstatics in previous ages assumed that God was intervening, for there was certainly no force in their conscious lives that could create such an experience. As we shall see in a later chapter, it may not be entirely wrong to say that God intervenes in an ecstatic experience, but one need not postulate some special individual act by the divinity.

Thus far in this chapter we have permitted social scientists to describe what mysticism is like. Now let us listen to some of the mystics themselves. F. C. Happold has written one of the best an-

[23] David Knowles, *The English Mystical Tradition*. London: Longmans, Todd, 1961, p. 3.

thologies of mysticism presently available.[24] He describes four such experiences in his life:

It happened in my room in Peterhouse on the evening of 1 February 1913, when I was an undergraduate at Cambridge. If I say that Christ came to me I should be using conventional words which would carry no precise meaning; for Christ comes to men and women in different ways. When I tried to record the experience at the time I used the imagery of the vision of the Holy Grail; it seemed to me to be like that. There was, however, no sensible vision. There was just the room, with its shabby furniture and the fire burning in the grate and the red-shaded lamp on the table. But the room was filled by a Presence, which in a strange way was both about me and within me, like light or warmth. I was overwhelmingly possessed by Someone who was not myself, and yet I felt I was more myself than I had ever been before. I was filled with an intense happiness, and almost unbearable joy, such as I had never known before and have never known since. And over all was a deep sense of peace and security and certainty.

Some experiences of this sort, which I have found recorded, lasted a very short time. Mine lasted several hours. What time I went to bed I do not know, but when I awoke in the morning it was still there. During the day it faded. It was very wonderful and quite unforgettable.

Though I now recognize the experience as of the kind described by the mystics, at that time I knew nothing of mysticism. . . .

The other experience of which I must tell, happened a little later in the same room. I have always thought of it as a continuation and completion of that I have described; it "felt" the same. This time, however, it seemed that a voice was speaking to me. It was not sensibly audible; it spoke within me. The words were strange: "Those who sought the city found the wood: and those who sought the wood found the city." Put into cold print they sound nonsensical. Yet I felt vividly that they meant something very important, that they were the key to a secret.

I shall have more to say of this second experience; but first I would tell of two others. The first of these occurred in late 1916, during the Battle of the Somme. I crouched in the darkness in a front-line trench, which was nothing but a muddy ditch, stinking with unburied corpses, amid a tangle of shell-holes. At dawn my battalion was due to attack. I watched the slow movement of the luminous dial of my wrist-watch, dreading the moment when I must get up and lead my men forward towards the German lines. And suddenly, with absolute certainty, I knew that I was utterly safe. It was not Rupert Brooke's:

> Safe though all safety's lost, safe where men fall;
> And if these poor limbs die, safest of all.

Still less was it the sort of fatalism not uncommon among fighting men in action. Rather it was a vivid sense of being completely safe physically. When the thunder of the barrage broke I went forward quite unafraid.

Baldly set down, the experience may not sound very important; it may be thought to have been merely the effect of a particularly heavy strain. It must be considered side by side with another experience which happened to me on the evening of 18 April 1936, the evening of the day before my son was born. My first child had been still-born and, as I lay in bed, I was very anxious about my wife and much disturbed in mind. And then a great peace came over me. I was conscious of a lovely, unexplainable pattern in the whole texture of things, a pattern of which everyone and everything was a part; and weaving the pattern was a Power; and that Power was what we faintly call Love. I realized that we are not lonely atoms in a cold, unfriendly, indifferent universe, but that each of us is linked up in a rhythm, of which we may be unconscious, and which we can never really know, but to which we can submit ourselves trustfully and unreservedly.[25]

Happold, mind you, was a very commonsensical British headmaster, a hero awarded a DSO for service during the First World War, and a quintessential Anglo-Saxon—not the sort who would be given to flim-flam. Nor was John Buchan, British novelist and diplomat, exactly what we would consider a mystical type. Yet:

I had been ploughing all day in the black dust of the Lichtenburg roads, and had come very late to a place called the Eye of Malmani—Malmani Oog—the spring of a river which presently loses itself in the Kalahari. We watered our horses and went supperless to bed. Next morning I bathed in one of the Malmani pools—and icy cold it was—and then basked in the early sunshine while breakfast was cooking. The water made a pleasant

[25] F. C. Happold, *Adventure in Search of a Creed*. London: Faber and Faber, 1955. Quotations reprinted by permission of Faber and Faber Ltd.

music, and near by was a covert of willows filled with singing birds. Then and there came on me the hour of revelation, when, though savagely hungry, I forgot about breakfast. Scents, sights, and sounds blended into a harmony so perfect that it transcended human expression, even human thought. It was like a glimpse of the peace of eternity.[26]

The moments of ecstasy can come in strange places—particularly for Englishmen, it seems: drab rooms, African landscapes, and even on a cricket field:

The thing happened one summer afternoon, on the school cricket field, while I was sitting on the grass, waiting my turn to bat. I was thinking about nothing in particular, merely enjoying the pleasures of midsummer idleness. Suddenly, and without warning, something invisible seemed to be drawn across the sky, transforming the world about me into a kind of tent of concentrated and enhanced significance. What had been merely an outside become an inside. The objective was somehow transformed into a completely subjective fact, which was experienced as "mine," but on a level where the word had no meaning; for "I" was no longer the familiar ego. Nothing more can be said about the experience, it brought no accession of knowledge about anything except, very obscurely, the knower and his way of knowing. After a few minutes there was a "return to normalcy." The event made a deep impression on me at the time; but, because it did not fit into any of the thought patterns—religious, philosophical, scientific —with which, as a boy of fifteen, I was familiar, it came to seem more and more anomalous, more and more irrelevant to "real life," and was finally forgotten.[27]

Happold, Buchan, and the young cricket player are in the finest tradition of British mysticism, a tradition forgotten after the Reformation. Walter Hilton, Julian of Norwich, the author of *The Cloud of Unknowing*, and, above all, Richard Rolle, a fascinating late-medieval English mystic, produced a mystical literature which can compare with any in the world, as is clear from Rolle's poetic description in *The Fire of Love*:

[26] Happold, *op. cit.*, p. 131. Quoted from John Buchan, *Memory Hold-the-Door*. London: Hodder and Stoughton,

[27] Happold, *op. cit.*, p. 130. Quoted from Margaret Isherwood, *The Root of the Matter*. London: Gollancz,

O honeyed flame, sweeter than all sweet, delightful beyond all creation!

My God, my Love, surge over me, pierce me by your love, wound me
with your beauty.

Surge over me, I say, who am longing for your comfort.

Reveal your healing medicine to your poor lover.

See, my one desire is for you; it is you my heart is seeking.

My soul pants for you; my whole being is athirst for you.

Yet you will not show yourself to me; you look away; you bar the
door, shun me, pass me over;

You even laugh at my innocent sufferings.

And yet you snatch your lovers away from all earthly things.

You lift them above every desire for worldly matters.

You make them capable of loving you—
    and love you they do indeed.

So they offer you their praise in spiritual song
    which bursts out from that inner fire;
    they know in truth the sweetness of the dart of love.

Ah, eternal and most lovable of all joys,
    you raise us from the very depths,
    and entrance us with the sight of divine majesty so often!

Come into me, Beloved!

All ever I had I have given up for you;
    I have spurned all that was to be mine,
    that you might make your home in my heart,
    and I your comfort.

Do not forsake me now, smitten with such great longing,
    whose consuming desire is to be amongst those who love you.

Grant me to love you,
    to rest in you,
    that in your kingdom I may be worthy
    to appear before you world without end.[28]

Mystics have often fallen back onto poetry to describe their experiences. There is no better ecstasy than John of the Cross's famous
*En una noche oscura,* one of the most dazzling poems ever produced
by humankind.

[28] Translated into modern English by Clifton Wolters. Middlesex, England:
Penguin Books, 1972, p. 45. © 1972 by Clifton Wolters. Reprinted by permission
of Penguin Books Ltd.

Upon a gloomy night,
With all my cares to loving ardours flushed,
 (O venture of delight!)
With nobody in sight
I went abroad when all my house was hushed.

In safety, in disguise,
In darkness up the secret stair I crept,
 (O happy enterprise!)
Concealed from other eyes,
When all my house at length in silence slept.

Upon a lucky night
In secrecy, inscrutable to sight,
I went without discerning
And with no other light
Except for that which in my heart was burning.

It lit and led me through
More certain than the light of noonday clear
To where One waited near
Whose presence well I knew,
There where no other presence might appear.

Oh night that was my guide!
Oh darkness dearer than the morning's pride,
Oh night that joined the lover
To the beloved bride
Transfiguring them each into the other.

Within my flowering breast
Which only for himself entire I save
He sank into his rest
And all my gifts I gave
Lulled by the airs with which the cedars wave.

Over the ramparts fanned
While the fresh wind was fluttering his tresses,
With his serenest hand
My neck he wounded, and
Suspended every sense with its caresses.

Lost to myself I stayed
My face upon my lover having laid
From all endeavour ceasing:

And all my cares releasing
Threw them among the lilies there to fade.[29]

Before John of the Cross, both Augustine and Bernard had similar experiences:

Thus with the flash of one trembling glance it [the soul] arrived at THAT WHICH IS. And then I saw Thy invisible things understood by the things that are made. But I could not fix my gaze thereon; and my infirmity being struck back, I was thrown again on my wonted habits, carrying along with me only a loving memory thereof, and a longing for what I had, as it were, perceived the odour of, but was not yet able to feed on. (Augustine, *Confessions*)

By what way then did He enter? Can it be that He did not enter at all, because He did not come from outside? for He is not one of the things that are without. Yet again, He did not come from within me, for He is good, and I know that *no good thing dwelleth in me.* I have gone up to the highest that I have, and behold, the Word was towering yet higher. My curiosity took me to the lowest depth to look for Him, nevertheless He was found still deeper. If I looked outside me, I found He was beyond my farthest; if I looked within He was more inward still. (St. Bernard, *Sermons on the Song of Songs.*)

And in more recent times, Simone Weil, a Jewish mystic who stood on the margins of Catholicism, remaining just outside, and Teilhard de Chardin, a French Jesuit who stood on the margins of Catholicism, remaining just on the inside, offer conclusive evidence that mysticism does not prevent one from being immersed in the problems of the world. Simone Weil describes what happened sometimes when she said her customary "Our Father" in Greek while working in the vineyard:

At times the very first words tear my thoughts from my body and transport it to a place outside space where there is neither perspective nor point

[29] Roy Campbell's translation of "En una noche oscura," printed in his *The Poems of St John of the Cross*. London: Harvill Press and Penguin Classics, 1963. Its full title is "Songs of the soul in rapture at having arrived at the height of perfection, which is union with God by the road of spiritual negation." Reprinted by permission of Hughes Massie Limited.

of view. The infinity of the ordinary expanses of perception is replaced by an infinity to the second or sometimes the third degree. At the same time, filling every part of this infinity of infinity, there is a silence, a silence which is not an absence of sound but which is the object of a positive sensation, more positive than that of sound. Noises, if there are any, only reach me after crossing the silence.

Sometimes, also, during this recitation or at other moments, Christ is present with me in person, but his presence is infinitely more real, more moving, more clear than on the first occasion he took possession of me.[30]

And Teilhard de Chardin:

. . . the coming of His Kingdom as I see it in my dreams. I mean the "implosive" encounter in human consciousness of the "ultra-human" and the "Christic" impulses—or, as I often express, of the Forward (i.e. the progress of mankind by "convergence") and the Upward (the spiritual ascent of mankind towards Christ, in whom it will find its completion and consummation, when, in St. Paul's words, God will be "all in all"). I am more and more convinced—judging from my own infinitesimal experience—that this process is indeed possible, and is actually in operation, and that it will psychologically transfigure the world of tomorrow.[31]

One can even find accounts of ecstatic interludes in fiction on occasion. Happold cites a passage from Anya Seton's novel, *The Winship Woman*:

A ray of sunshine started down between the tree trunks. It touched the pool with liquid gold. The pool became transparent to its green depths and her self was plunged in those depths and yet upraised with joy upon the rushing wind. The light grew stronger and turned white. In this crystal whiteness there was ecstasy. Against the light she saw a wren fly by; the wren was made of rhythm, it flew with meaning, with a radiant meaning. There was the same meaning in the caterpillar as it inched along the rock, and the moss, and the little nuts which had rolled across the leaves.

And still the apperception grew, and the significance. The significance

---

30 Happold, *op. cit.*, p. 142. Quoted from Simone Weil, *Waiting on God*, Emma Cranford (Trans.). London: Routledge and Kegan Paul.

31 Happold, *op. cit.*, p. 366. Quoted from *Letters from a Traveller*. London: Collins, and New York: Harper & Row.

was bliss, it made a created whole of everything she watched and touched and heard—and the essence of this created whole was love. She felt love pouring from the light, it bathed her with music and with perfume; the love was far off at the source of the light, and yet it drenched her through. And the source and she were one.

The minutes passed. The light moved softly down, and faded from the pool. The ecstasy diminished, it quietened, but in its stead came a serenity and sureness she had never known.[32]

Finally, two contemporary American poets prove that even in the city of Chicago, county of Cook, state of Illinois, the mystical light still shines:

### PRAYER OF SOMEONE WHO HAS BEEN THERE BEFORE

After the last time
    when I finally turned from flight
    and from somewhere came the strength
        to go back
I rummaged the ruins
    a refugee picking through bombed belongings
      for what surely was destroyed
and began again.
When a child tests the ice for skating,
he checks for thickness not for smoothness.
He will endure the bumps
as long as he does not drown.
      Out of fear of falling in
      I grew my new life
        thick and rough
        with an alarm system on the heart
        and an escape hatch in the head.
It was as spontaneous
as a military campaign.
    I love in small amounts
      like a sick man sipping whiskey.

[32] Happold, *op. cit.*, pp. 90–91.

Hope was sensibly bracketed. Is there any other way?
    Each day was lived within its limits.
      Each joy swallowed quickly.
    Perhaps it was not all-out embracement
                      of life—
          the position of crucifixion—
    but neither was it the hunched
      and jabbing stance of the boxer.
There was courtesy     and consideration
and manners.
It was not that bad.
    What's more—it was necessary.
    What's important—it was mine.
Now this.
This thing     this feeling
    This unpardonable intrusion
      which had no part to play
      but played it anyway
All those things scrupulously screened out
                want in.
And I can sense it coming,
    a second coming,
    a second shattering.
    Someone   Something  is at me once more,
      mocking my defenses,
      wrenching my soul.
        God damn it!
Is it you again, Lord? [33]

And the same theme of an experience repeated is echoed by another Chicago Irishwoman:

### PATHFINDING

Lord Lord, take me again out out into the wilderness
I'll not be in terror of the wind.
Join me with the global spin

[33] Unpublished poem by John Shea. Used by permission of the author.

the better to wink at land and seas traveling with me.
Caught up in wonder,
fleeing from the everyman of my soul
    towards my own creation—that new face, distinct—
and sharing with the universe our gifts
traversing terrain never seen by my eyes
but run through my sight—belief
Oh yes, get it—true seeing, humor beyond
    mind and imagination
and more contagious than the common cold.
Ah, hold the flesh nestled into your air,
cradle this baby born me,
double the sounds and send me off down the river rapids
bumping round,
blowing bubbles with the most ferocious wakes.
Bake me, burn me with sun so yellow
I feel for the shadow on my fellow man's back
and clap for the daffodils, thrill at the praise they give
    living through the rainstorm
glorious again, lifting heads so rich with golden drops!
    Flip flop—over there a pear, trying for ripeness
    Eager for the bite,
    Reaching to be juice on teeth.
Oh never never land of Peter Pan
never was and never shall be but is
        His!
Where war is a bore we have no need
    except to breathe with the fuzz on violets leaves,
    kissing whiskered cheeks of loved ones,
And know that something, everything is true.
A bleeding joy in tears, that the secret lies open
    and blessings are forever.[34]

It is worth emphasizing that none of the mystics quoted above
were either psychotics or dropouts. Augustine was a bishop, Bernard
an abbot, Richard Rolle an active pastor, Happold a schoolmaster,
John Buchan became governor general of Canada, Teilhard de

[34] Unpublished poem by Nancy G. McCready. Used by permission of the
author.

Chardin was a paleontologist, John of the Cross reformed a religious order. They did not withdraw from the world; they did not give up ordinary activities; much less did any of them show any particular sign that they needed psychotherapy. Their mystical visions may very well have formed their lives; indeed, some make it quite explicit that their lives were transformed, a transformation that was not unbalanced or abnormal. In fact a good case might be made for the assertion that the mystics we have quoted were more "normal" than anyone else around them.

# CHAPTER THREE

# The Psychology of Ecstasy

Richard Rolle begins the prologue of his *Fire of Love* with the following paragraph:

I cannot tell you how surprised I was the first time I felt my heart begin to warm. It was real warmth, too, not imaginary, and it felt as if it were actually on fire. I was astonished at the way the heat surged up, and how this new sensation brought great and unexpected comfort. I had to keep feeling my breast to make sure there was no physical reason for it! But once I realized that it came entirely from within, that this fire of love had no cause, material or sinful, but was the gift of my Maker, I was absolutely delighted, and wanted my love to be even greater. And this longing was all the more urgent because of the delightful effect and the interior sweetness which this spiritual flame fed into my soul. Before the infusion of this comfort I had never thought that we exiles could possibly have known such warmth, so sweet was the devotion it kindled. It set my soul aglow as if a real fire was burning there.[1]

For Rolle this was all that was necessary—the fire, the warmth, the heat he experienced came from contact with his Maker. However, in our far more sophisticated era, knowing what we do about the human unconscious, we are predisposed to seek some psychological explanation for the mystical experience. John White, in his book *The Highest State of Consciousness*, has gathered together a collection of such explanations. It is interesting and at times helpful reading, especially since the psychoanalytically oriented student of mysticism simply cannot escape the notion that mysticism is a form of madness or at least is related to it. R. D. Laing, that rather peculiar Scottish psychiatrist who believes that all sane people are mad and all mad people sane, suggests that when a child adapts to this world he "abdicates his capacity for ecstasy. ('L'enfant abdique son extase': Mallarmé.)" [2] His patients, Laing argues, are mad because of the destruction worked on them by us, the society around them. True sanity is to be obtained only by the "dissolution of the normal ego, that false self completely adjusted to our alienated social reality. . . ." [3] The mystical experience, then, represents the "emergence of the 'inner' archetypal mediators of divine power, and through this death a rebirth, and the eventual re-establishment of a new kind of ego-functioning, the ego now being the servant of the divine, no longer its betrayer." [4]

Whether Laing believes in a God that is anything like the God of the Christians is problematic, but for him ecstasy is a form of madness because only the "madman" has the courage to break with the insanity of the contemporary world. All this is very edifying and very radical, but hardly very informative about the nature of the ecstatic experience.

---

[1] Richard Rolle, *The Fire of Love*. Translated into modern English by Clifton Wolters. Middlesex, England: Penguin Books, 1972, p. 45. © 1972 by Clifton Wolters. Reprinted by permission of Penguin Books Ltd.

[2] R. D. Laing, "Transcendental Experience," in John White, *op. cit.*, p. 112.

[3] *Ibid.*, p. 113.

[4] *Ibid.*, p. 113.

Much more clinically precise are Raymond Prince and Charles Savage, who believe—as Laing implies with his quotation from Mallarmé—that ecstasy implies a regression into an infantile state. This regression is similar to psychosis but distinct from it: "A psychosis is a pressured withdrawal with—in many cases—an incomplete return. A mystical state is a controlled withdrawal and return; a death and rebirth, often a rebirth into a world with a radical shift in its iconography—a death and transfiguration." [5]

The two authors contend that in the regression experience a person may very well go back to the very earliest sensations of childhood when there was practically no boundary between self and world. Only as the infant begins to grow up does he perceive that his own body is physically distinct from the surrounding environment. The ecstatic experience is a form of regression to that state of infancy in which the person experiences once again that primal intimacy in union with his mother's breast. Hence, according to Prince and Savage, the Oriental mandala symbol is frequently used in Eastern religions as a trigger for the mystical interlude precisely because it calls to mind the mother's breast.

Kenneth Wapnick suggests a similarity between mysticism and schizophrenia. The schizophrenic, too, is illumined by a special light from the inner world, and also in the name of this light rejects the outer world of everyday life. Escape from the outer world to the inner world is deemed madness in the schizophrenic, because he is unable to return to the outer world, while the mystic, on the other hand, returns to the outer world and involves himself in it once again. Wapnick says:

. . . the mystic's life may be seen as a recognition of the existence of the inner, personal experience, which though independnt of, and even antagonistic to, the social reality, cannot be fully developed unless the individual also affirms his role in society. Beautiful and powerful feelings are not sufficient to improve one's functioning in the social world. What is needed is the integration of these inner experiences with the various social roles one adopts. The mystic provides the example of the method

[5] Raymond Prince and Charles Savage, "Mystical States and the Concept of Regression," in John White, *op. cit.*, p. 132.

whereby the inner and outer may be joined; the schizophrenic, the tragic result when they are separated.[6]

Roland Fischer devises an elaborate diagram, which we reproduce here, to show that mystical rapture is at one end of a continuum with a Yoga trance at the other. Normal daily perception ranges in between the two. As one moves from normal daily perception toward ecstasy, one experiences an increasingly higher state of perceptual arousal.

These states are experienced in terms of increasing data content and increasing rate of data processing, and may result in a *creative* (artistic or religious) state. Eventually, however, the rate of processing cannot keep step with the ever-increasing data content—"the torrential flood of inner sensation"—and results in the schizophrenic "jammed computer" state. At the peak of *ecstatic* states, there is no data content from without, and, therefore, no rate of data processing from within, the only content of the experience at the height of rapture being the reflection of the mystic in his own "program." [7]

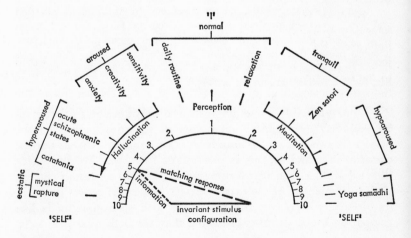

[6] Kenneth Wapnick, "Mysticism and Schizophrenia," in John White, *op. cit.,* p. 173.

[7] Roland Fischer, "On Creative, Psychotic and Ecstatic States," in White, *op. cit.,* p. 191.

Mysticism, then, may be schizophrenia, it may be regression, it may be a fouled-up internal computer program. However, Alexander Maven does them all one better.[8] He suggests that it is a regression not to infancy or the mother's breast, but to the experience of the sperm joining the ovum at the moment of conception. The ecstatic "breaking in" that the mystic experiences really is a recollection of the ecstasy of the sperm breaking into the ovum. One would have to go a long way to top that explanation!

It is hard to know what these authors mean. Are they speaking analogically? Are they saying that the mystical experience is *like* regression or schizophrenia or a jammed computer? If all they are doing is elaborating a metaphor, their insights may be helpful. If, on the other hand, they are suggesting that the mystical interlude is in fact "the same thing as" regression or schizophrenia or the jammed computer, then they are obviously wrong. It is quite clear that the mystical interlude is none of those entirely. Claire Myers Owens refutes psychiatric explanations of the mystical experience. She comments:

The mystic state, whether spontaneous or induced through meditation and other practices, produces a release of energy from the unconscious which permits the actualization of man's highest potentialities. Therefore, it seems proper that the mystic state be studied by science without prejudice, in an effort to discover whether it may indeed offer clues to the good life, for the individual and for society.[9]

Unquestionably, something extraordinary goes on in the mystical episode. A transformation occurs in the consciousness of the person. Regression and schizophrenia are departures from normal consciousness, and so, too, is the ecstatic interlude. To this extent they are similar. But it is a different kind of consciousness change, both in the nature of the experience for those who report it and in its aftereffects. To compare mysticism with schizophrenia is like comparing bread with steak because they are both foods.

[8] Alexander Maven, "The Mystic Union: A Suggested Biological Interpretation," in White, *op. cit.*, pp. 429–35.
[9] Claire Myers Owens, "The Mystical Experience: Facts and Values," in White, *op. cit.*, p. 152.

Arnold M. Ludwig lists ten characteristics of the altered state of consciousness (ASC), all of which seem to apply to mystical ecstasy:[10]

1. *Alterations in thinking.* Subjective disturbances in concentration, attention, memory, and judgment represent common findings. . . . The distinction between cause and effect becomes blurred, and ambivalence may be pronounced whereby incongruities or opposites may coexist without any logical conflict.

2. *Disturbed time sense.* Subjective feelings of timelessness, time coming to a standstill, the acceleration or slowing of time . . . are common.

3. *Loss of control.* As a person enters or is in an ASC, he often experiences fears of losing his grip on reality and losing his self-control.

4. *Change in emotional expression.* Emotional extremes, from ecstasy and orgiastic equivalents to profound fear and depression, commonly occur.

5. *Body image change.* There is . . . a common propensity for individuals to experience a profound sense of depersonalization, a schism between body and mind, feelings of derealization, or a dissolution of boundaries between self and others, the world, or universe.

6. *Perceptual distortions.* There may be the presence of perceptual aberrations, including hallucinations, pseudohallucinations, increased visual imagery, subjectively felt hyperacuteness of perception, and illusions of every variety.

7. *Change in meaning or significance.* There seems to be a predilection of people in these states to attach an increased meaning or significance to their subjective experience, ideas, or perceptions. At times, it appears as though the person is undergoing an attenuated "eureka" experience during which feelings of profound insight, illumination, and truth frequently occur.

8. *Sense of the ineffable.* Contributing to the sense of the ineffable is the tendency of persons to develop varying degrees of am-

10 Arnold M. Ludwig, "Altered States of Consciousness," Arch. Gen. Psychiat. Vol. 15, 1966, pp. 225–34. I have condensed his descriptions somewhat.

nesias for their experiences during profound alterations of consciousness.

9. *Feelings of rejuvenation.* Many persons claim to experience
a new sense of hope, rejuvenation, renaissance, or rebirth.

10. *Hypersuggestibility.* There is an increased susceptibility
and propensity of persons uncritically to accept and/or automatically to respond to specific statements . . . or nonspecific cues . . .
(or) to misperceive or misinterpret various stimuli or situations
based either on inner fears or wishes.

Dr. Ludwig's catalogue of characteristics of the altered state of
consciousness seems complete; all abound in the literature of the
ecstatic. His categories are presented in aloof and neutral terms, but
the net result of his view is to imply that the one on the "outside"
who watches the ecstatic is in touch with reality, while the ecstatic
has lost touch with it. Such, indeed, may be the case, but the mystic
would assert that what he sees is the really real and that everything
else is, if not illusion, at least not so clearly real.

Similarly, Ludwig suggests that ASC—including mystical ecstasy—has three adaptive functions: healing, new knowledge and
experience, and "the social function." The social function is especially interesting in his description:

From the individual's vantage point, possession by one of the tribal or
local deities or Holy Spirit during a religious ceremony would allow him
to attain high status through fulfilling his cult role, gain a temporary free-
dom of responsibility from his actions and pronouncements, or enable him
to act out in a socially sanctioned way his aggressive and sexual conflicts or
desires. Tensions and fears are dissipated, and a new sense of spiritual security and confidence may supplant the despair and hopelessness of a marginal existence.

From society's standpoint, the needs of the tribe or groups are met
through its vicarious identification with the entranced person who not only
derives individual satisfaction from divine possession but also acts out certain ritualized group conflicts and aspirations, such as the theme of death
and resurrection, cultural taboos, and so on. Moreover, the dramatic be-
havioral manifestations of spirit possession serve to convince the partic-
ipants of the continued personal interest of their gods, reaffirm their local

beliefs, allow them to exert some control over the unknown, enhance group cohesion and identification, and endow the utterances of the entranced person, shaman, or priest with an importance they might otherwise not have if spoken in an ordinary setting. In general, the existence of such practices represents an excellent example of how society creates modes of reducing frustration, stress and loneliness through group action.[11]

*Functional analysis* is an important technique in social science. Nevertheless, the rather simple functionalism of those two paragraphs from Ludwig would scarcely be acceptable to sociologists in 1973. The dispassionate prose of the functionalist, which allows him to appear removed from the human condition, is simply not tolerable to the younger generation of social researchers. Ecstasy may well reduce frustration, stress, and loneliness; it may dissipate fears and tensions and generate a new sense of spiritual security and confidence; it may ease the despair and hopelessness of a marginal existence. But it does not follow that that is what ecstasy is all about either for the ecstatic himself or for those with whom he interacts after his mystical experience. Much less is it reasonable to assume, as functional analysis frequently does, that the ecstatic and his fellows are somehow or other conspiring to arrive at socially adaptive functions. The mystic may be up to something else altogether, and the general reaction of those who have one on their hands is not to know what the hell to do with him. Efficiently administered families, schools, and congregations are hard put to cope with a mystic.

Arthur J. Deikman[12] uses the concept of deautomatization to explain the mystical experience. In ordinary daily life psychological processes by which we organize limits, and select and interpret the stimuli we experience, work automatically. We do not pause and reflect on each sensuous stimulus we experience. If it were necessary to be conscious of all our sensuous processes, we would have no time to do anything else. Deautomatization, then, is merely the "undoing" of automatization; that is, we begin to pay close attention to certain perceptual stimuli. The ordinary structure of our sensory

---

11 Ludwig, *op. cit.,* pp. 233–34.

12 "Deautomatization and the Mystic Experience," *Psychiatry,* Vol. 29, 1966, pp. 324–38. Reprinted in *Altered States of Consciousness,* Charles Tart (ed.). New York: Wiley & Sons, 1969, pp. 23–43.

processes breaks down or is "shaken up," and we become conscious of stimuli to which we had formerly paid no attention.

Deikman notes that automatization is absolutely essential for "maximum efficiency in achieving the basic goals of the individual: biological survival as an organism and psychological survival as a personality." [13] Under certain sets of circumstances, however, and Deikman mentions either acute psychosis or LSD states, we engage in "alternate modes of consciousness whose stimulus processing may be less efficient from a biological point of view but whose very inefficiency may permit the experience of aspects of the real world formerly excluded or ignored." [14] Such a shift, Deikman assures us, "is a function of the motivation of the individual, his particular neurophysiological state, and the environmental conditions encouraging or discouraging such a change." [15]

Deikman certainly describes a perceptual process that seems to occur in the ecstatic experience. But is ecstasy to be identified with a change in the modes of perception? The mystics report that their perception does indeed change, but to them the important element is what they perceive in this new mode of perception, not the alteration of the perception.

Deikman seems to understand this when he says, "The mystic vision is one of unity, and modern physics lends some support to this perception when it asserts that the world and its living forms are variations of the same elements." Nevertheless, Deikman seems confident that it is not something outside (God) but something inside (the unconscious) that is what the mystic perceives, "an internal perception, an experience that can be ecstatic, profound, or therapeutic for purely internal reasons." [16]

Indeed, the question of whether it is the world outside or the world inside that the mystic intuits seems scarcely to be the point. The mystic himself tells us that it is both, that he perceives himself as part of the world outside and the world "outside" as profoundly and intimately part of him. By creating a dichotomy between the

13 *Ibid.*, p. 43.
14 *Ibid.*, p. 44.
15 *Ibid.*, p. 43.
16 *Ibid.*, p. 45.

two, Deikman, perhaps unintentionally, seems to be thinking of the human person as Descartes' thinking machine inside a body, when it is precisely the distinction between the subject knowing and the object known that the mystic proclaims has been temporarily suspended. Like many psychological researchers, Deikman is incapable of conceding that what goes on in ecstasy is what the mystic says goes on: a dramatically different form of cognition. Deikman tells us how the senses operate in this alternate form of cognition, but he does not seem interested in the cognition itself.

There is, of course, a rhetorical style that is appropriate to social research. Even the most enthusiastic ethnomethodologist tries to maintain some distance between himself and the perceptions he reports. Yet, one is forced to the observation that none of the psychological perspectives that I have described in this chapter seems to do justice to the paragraph from Richard Rolle with which this chapter begins. It is not that psychological theories distort Rolle's experience; but one can say that they do not seem to comprehend it. They all describe some of the things that apparently go on in an interlude of mystical ecstasy, but they do not describe the ecstasy at all. This is primarily, I suspect, because they are not prepared to concede that mystics like Rolle may very well know more about reality than any psychologist or psychiatrist does. I am not suggesting that this is certainly the case, but it seems to me that the psychological study of mysticism will begin when psychologists are willing to concede the possibility that mystics may indeed know something about the Way Things Are. The mystic can only be understood by a psychologist who will approach him with both respect and sympathy and not merely with curiosity.

One of the troubles with psychological explanations of mysticism is that they ignore the social and cultural context. In his various writings Mircea Eliade provides just such a context. For him, religious experience is "an experience of existence in its totality, which reveals to a man his own mode of being in the World." [17] Religion "shows forth *that which really is*," and "religion 'begins' when and where there is a total revelation or reality; a revelation

[17] Mircea Eliade, *Myths, Dreams, and Mysteries*. New York: Harper & Row. A Harper Torchbook, 1967, p. 17.

which is at once that of the sacred—of that which supremely *is*, of what is neither illusory nor evanescent—and of man's relationship to the sacred, a relationship which is multiple, changing, sometimes ambivalent, but which always places man at the very heart of the real." [18]

The religious experience and the mystical experience, which is the religious experience par excellence, are breaking-throughs to that which supremely *is*. That which supremely *is* exists in a different time frame from the "profane duration" that is the prime pattern of our everyday life. Primitive rituals, which were always religious experiences and frequently ones of collective ecstasy, were attempts to become present in the great world-ordering events which marked the Beginnings:

. . . we know that the initiation of a transhuman model, the repetition of an exemplary scenario and the breakaway from profane time through a moment which opens out into the Great Time, are the essential marks of "mythical behavior"—that is, the behavior of the man of the archaic societies, who finds the very source of his existence in the myth. One is always *contemporary with a myth*, during the time when one repeats it or imitates the gestures of the mythic personages.[19]

The ecstatic experience, then, from the point of view of the history of religion, is an attempt to recapture a Great Time, or primordial time, or mythical time by breaking away from the present time. It is, in Eliade's words, an "attempt to return to Paradise"; and the Paradise myth (along with its companion, the myth of the Noble Savage) is universal in the human condition, even in the modern human condition. In an analysis of both the Yoga and the psychoanalysis experience, Eliade argues that they, too, are attempts to return to Paradise, to recapture for the sake of personal growth the innocence and freedoms of the Beginning. Thus, when those primitive mystics of the Plains Indians, the shamans, go into one of their trances, they are trying to recapture Paradise; they are going out of ordinary time to recapture Real Time:

18 *Ibid.*, pp. 17–18.
19 *Ibid.*, p. 30.

The imitation of the cries of animals by the shamans, which has not failed to impress observers, and which ethnologists have often supposed to be the manifestation of a pathological *possession,* actually betokens the desire to recover friendship with the animals and thus enter into the primordial Paradise. The ecstatic trance, whatever its phenomenology may be, only appears as an aberration if we lose sight of its spiritual significance. In reality, as we saw, the shaman tried to reestablish the communications between Earth and Heaven that were interrupted by "the Fall." The mastery of fire, too, is no mere superstition of savages; on the contrary, it is a demonstration that the shaman partakes of the nature of *spirits.*[20]

And Eliade concludes with the comment that it is necessary to understand the meanings involved in a person's behavior if we are to be objective about that behavior—that is to say, the meanings *he* puts on it, and not the ones we impose:

To recall just one example: the imitation of the animals' cries. For more than a century it was thought that the strange cries of the shaman were a proof of his mental disequilibrium. But they were signs of something very different: of the nostalgia for Paradise which had haunted Isaiah and Virgil, which had nourished the saintliness of the Fathers of the Church, and that blossomed anew, victorious, in the life of St. Francis of Assisi.[21]

So there may be similarities between what goes on in ecstasy and what goes on in certain psychotic states. In both, ordinary time and place are suspended, but the ecstatic permits such a suspension to occur and the psychotic cannot control either his breaking away or his reentry. "The ecstasy re-actualizes, for a time, what was the initial state of mankind as a whole—except that the shaman no longer mounts up to Heaven in flesh and blood as the primordial man used to do, but only *in the spirit,* in the state of ecstasy." [22]

To summarize this chapter, the mystical experience seems to be reasonably common. It involves a breaking away from daily experience of time and place and a search for some sort of basic and primitive union with the Way Things Really Are. While in its ori-

20 *Ibid.,* pp. 71–72.
21 *Ibid.,* p. 72.
22 *Ibid.,* p. 98.

gins it was certainly religious, it need not be religious for people today, in the sense that it need not have a special theological or denominational context. However, in its attempt to come to grips experientially with the Way Things Really Are, the mystical interlude is implicitly and fundamentally religious. It may look like certain forms of mental illness, because when it occurs the boundaries between self and the rest of reality are blurred and because the ordinary state of consciousness is temporarily replaced by something much different. It is usually triggered by some sort of experience of goodness, truth, beauty, or pleasure that apparently predisposes the person for the mystical event by taking his mind off ordinary events and making him temporarily passive so that "reality may rush in." When that rushing in occurs, the person has the sense of being seized by something "demonic" (in Rollo May's sense of something that takes control of the whole personality). Peace, joy, union, insight, love, confidence seem to take possession of the person. If the context of the experience is Christian, there also seems to come a reassurance of personal survival; if the context is Eastern, the dominant impression may be one of union, of being merged with a great cosmic reality. Finally, the ecstatic "comes down" from his moments of rapture with new serenity and confidence for his everyday life.

# CHAPTER FOUR

# Mysticism and Creative Experience

In this chapter and the next, I shall contend that the mystical experience is a *natural* form of knowledge in the sense that one need postulate no special intervention of the deity to explain it. Nevertheless, in the mystic experience the person makes *contact* with the Way Things Are.

While the mystical insight is a natural way of knowing, it does not follow that it is an ordinary way of knowing. Everyone may have the capacity for such insight, though most will probably never experience it; those who do may experience it rarely. For reasons of both nature and nurture there are relatively few mystics who have frequent ecstatic experiences (although there are many more than we would have assumed before our national survey data became available). Everyone can put musical notes on paper, but Mozarts appear rarely.

Ronald Shor, focusing primarily on hypnotism, developed a number of notions that are relevant to mystic experiences.[1] Like Deikman, Shor notes the automatic or quasi-automatic operation of our ordinary perceptual and cognitive lives. He calls it "the generalized-reality orientation." Shor states that this usual state of consciousness "is characterized by the mobilization of a structured frame of reference in the background of attention which supports, interprets, and gives meaning to all experiences."[2] This generalized-reality orientation requires constant active mental effort, but it is usually not consciously or explicitly directive. It is developed slowly throughout the life cycle, and is flexible and shifting, depending on the requirements of a given situation. A trance occurs when the generalized-reality orientation has faded into unawareness, though it does not fade completely. In the so-called trance state "(a) experiences cannot have their usual meanings; (b) experiences may have special meanings which result from their isolation from the totality of general experiences; and (c) special orientations or special tasks can function temporarily as the only possible reality for the subject in his phenomenal awareness as a result of their isolation from the totality of general experience."[3]

Hence for Shor a good hypnotic subject is a person who has the ability to give up voluntarily his usual reality orientation and who can build up a special orientation to reality which becomes the only one for him in his trance experience. One might say that, similarly, a good mystic is one who can suspend his generalized-reality orientation and concentrate on something else.

But the question is, on what is he concentrating? It is surely not his everyday experience, but it does not therefore follow that it is unreal. We can make Shor's position acceptable to us and to the mystics whom we are trying to understand if we say that when the generalized-reality orientation is suspended in the mystic experience

[1] Ronald Shor, "Hypnosis and the Concept of the Generalized Reality-Orientation," *American Journal of Psychotherapy*, Vol. 13, 1959, pp. 582–602. Reprinted in Charles T. Tart, *op. cit.*, pp. 233–50.

[2] Shor in Tart, *op. cit.*, p. 236.

[3] *Ibid.*, p. 245.

there follows a concentration on a specialized-reality orientation. And now the question is whether the generalized orientation is suspended first and then attention focused on the specialized orientation, or whether it is, as the mystics claim, the specialized orientation "rushing in," taking possession of them, and excluding at least for a few brief moments the generalized-reality orientation.

In other words, does the trance cause the mystical insight (preceding it at least) or does the mystical insight produce trance? If one reads the accounts of the mystics carefully, there seems to be some evidence that in many cases there is a drift of consciousness and perception which eases the focus of ordinary awareness. Generalized-reality orientation can slow down a bit for a person experiencing powerfully one of the "triggers" of the mystic interlude—those works of nature, man, and God so often mentioned by those who have experienced ecstasy. There may be a relaxation of the generalized-reality orientation, but that is hardly a trance. The relatively complete suspension of the automatic perceptive processes seems to occur simultaneously with the mystic insight and with such power and force that the outside observer can assert that one causes the other only because of his own dogmatic preconceptions.

I would like to suggest that an appropriate analogue for the mystical experience is neither schizophrenia nor regression but rather the creative process.[4] By the creative process I do not mean the producing of a painting, a symphony, or a book; I mean that process of mind by which the musician perceives the entire symphony before he begins to work, the novelist intuits his story before he sets a word on paper, by which the painter looks at a scene and "sees" what he is going to paint. The work of executing the creation is simply the task of molding the materials of one's art so that they approximate the insight and the vision that preexist the work itself.

Prose essays, I will concede, represent a fairly low level of artistic ability, and yet as a writer of such essays I am quite conscious that when I do my best writing I have the basic *insight* or *gestalt*

---

4 In this discussion I lean heavily on two rather disparate sources—Lawrence S. Kubie, *Neurotic Distortion of the Creative Process*. New York: Noonday Press, 1961; and Jacques Maritain, *Art and Scholasticism* and *Creative Intuition in Art and Poetry*. New York: World Publishing, 1955.

or pattern in mind not only before I sit down at the typewriter but before I set a word of outline on paper. I *know* what I want to say, and I know it in a brief flash of insight. There is still much hard work to be done, but it is obedient to the outline or the vision of the essay that I had before I began. There are times when I see entire books in such flashes of insight. It may take six months to a year to do the research necessary to flesh out the insight, but the insight came first. I might add that even in such a relatively unartistic activity as writing nonfiction prose the insight is a heavy burden to carry around until it is lightened by filling it out with words. The intellectual process is completely different from ordinary discursive reasoning, and I might add that it is also completely different from the process I engage in when writing straight social science commentary on statistical tables. The only way I can describe what happens is that when I have a clear and powerful insight, and I am writing with attention to it, the words fairly dance on the page before me. I say things I am not conscious of ever having thought before, in ways that surprise me. There is something special going on in my mind during these periods; but I would submit that my mind is not creating the reality that I try to describe, but that it is rather intuiting a reality outside. Or to leave aside the Cartesianism of contemporary perceptual psychology, I am not describing something that goes on inside myself, I am describing something that I see in the world *out there*.

Jacques Maritain suggests that what is at work in the creative process is the "agent intellect" (or, in the Latin of the Scholastics, the *intellectus agens*). The agent intellect is a restless, roving, energetic, prowling, suspicious, intrigued, curious, sensitive capacity of the mind that is driven to seek out reality. It is a largely unconscious form of intellectual activity in the sense that it is not discursive, not formal, not logical; it is the human person, grasping for the real.

Leonard Kubie calls the same kind of "knowing" the "preconscious":

There is however another type of mentation whose relationship to its roots is figurative and allegorical. The function of this intermediate form of mentation is to express at least by implication the nuances of thought and feeling, those collateral and emotional references which cluster around the central core of meaning. Here every coded signal has many overlapping meanings; and every item of data from the world of experience has many coded representatives. This is the form of coded language that is essential for all creative thinking, whether in art or science.[5]

In Kubie's thought the preconscious is the place where images and symbols frolic and dance, forming and reforming patterns. "Preconscious processes are not circumscribed by the more pedestrian and literal restrictions of conscious language."[6] On the contrary, neurotic distortion does not silence the preconscious; it is precisely in the kaleidoscopic juxtaposition of images that insight is born:

These approximate less closely the limited one-to-one relationships of the fully matured language of conscious symbolic functions, but retain a broader overlapping base of multiple meanings. This enables them to use the symbolic process in a more allegorical and figurative fashion. In the adult who is not hamstrung by conscious or unconscious fear and guilt, preconscious processes make free use of analogy and allegory, superimposing dissimilar ingredients into new perceptual and conceptual patterns, thus reshuffling experience to achieve that fantastic degree of condensation without which creativity in any field of activity would be impossible. In the preconscious use of imagery and allegory many experiences are condensed into a single hieroglyph, which expresses in one symbol far more than one can say slowly and precisely, word by word, on the fully conscious level. This is why preconscious mentation is the Seven-League Boot of intuitive creative functions. This is how and why preconscious condensations are used in poetry, humor, the dream, and the symptom.[7]

In the preconscious intellect one is constantly shuffling, sorting, arranging and rearranging the various images and symbols that have been absorbed from life's experience. In dreams, trances, and the creative process, the workings of the preconscious intellect are permitted to come into consciousness, and one becomes aware that at some level of the personality one has perceived connections and

[5] Kubie, *op. cit.*, pp. 30–31.
[6] *Ibid.*, p. 34.
[7] *Ibid.*, pp. 34–35.

linkages that had never been noticed before. One level of the mind has been wrestling with reality in a poetic fashion, that is to say, in a symbol-manipulation fashion, while the rest of the mind has scarcely noticed. The artistic-creative process is, quite simply, one in which this deeper level of "knowing" is permitted to become conscious and "do its own thing." Yet the power and ingenuity of the preconscious intellect (or *intellectus agens*) is so great that it is not surprising that one frequently has the feeling of "being taken possession of" by some outside force.

I am not arguing that the ecstatic interlude is the same as the creative process, or even that it is necessarily in the preconscious intellect that the ecstatic experience finds its origin. I am suggesting rather that there are many levels of human cognition, some of which are not ordinarily conscious. When some of these levels become conscious one has the experience of being "taken possession of" by an outside power. And in a way one has been, because a communication link has been set up between the outside world and the deeper processes of the personality of which the conscious intellect is not normally aware. When this link between reality and the depths of the personality becomes explicit, the generalized-reality orientation (the conscious intellect, the automatic structure of perception—whatever we call it) is temporarily swept aside—though as Shor points out, never completely. But if the creative process is a fair analogue to the mystical experience, it follows that what is important about the experience is not that it is a change in "feeling state" or the advent of trance, although that is what the outside observer may notice. These may be effects, or at least correlates, of a new, more powerful and more basic form of *"knowing"* that has begun to operate. In Shor's terminology, it is a "new special orientation toward reality which temporarily becomes the only possible reality." [8] It takes place in both the creative process and in the ecstatic interlude. For the creative artist this special reality rarely deprives him of his capacity to deal also, however imperfectly, with generalized reality. For the mystic, at least during the interlude of ecstasy, generalized reality is tuned out almost entirely. Hence the

[8] Shor, *op. cit.*, p. 247.

mystic seems to be in a trance, while the creative artist does not, though he may frequently appear preoccupied.

The important contribution Shor has made to our thinking is the assertion that it is indeed reality (though a special one) with which the person in a trance is engaged. Whether the reality that the mystic and the creative artist seem to see is more or less "real" than that which the uncreative and unmystic experience in their daily lives is a matter of debate. The unmystical psychologist and the uncreative observer of a Picasso painting may be inclined to think that there is something mad about this special reality. To which the mystic and the artist respond that what is really mad is their not seeing how special their reality really is.

The ecstatic, like the artist, is not denying the validity of ordinary experience. He claims that his experience enables him to get beyond the appearances of ordinary experience and knowledge, however valid those appearances may be. He perceives the substance of things, their essence, The Way Things Are. The artist may be wrong, and many are; the mystic may be wrong, and surely many are; but if one is to deal with artists and mystics with any kind of understanding, one must accept as a point of discussion their assertion that they have seen something real. To merely analyze their feeling states and to treat the descriptions of their experiences as a form of delusion is to make up one's mind for a priori and doctrinaire reasons.

It is also to assume that ordinary discursive reasoning—supported by empirical evidence, it is hoped—is the only valid kind. This rules out not only the ecstatic but the poet, the prophet, the philosopher, the theologian, the metaphysician, as well as the common sense of the ordinary man, which frequently cannot be validated either. Once one concedes the possibility that there may be intuitive, nondiscursive forms of knowledge, then one must logically accept the possibility that the mystical insight is indeed a way of knowing. And if it is a way of knowing, then what the mystic knows —or claims to know—becomes a matter of prime importance.

# CHAPTER FIVE

# Ecstasy as Knowledge

In this chapter I shall attempt my own tentative explanation of what happens in the mystical interlude. I scarcely intend it as a definitive description, but more as a model which may be useful for understanding some of the reality of the ecstatic experience. I will assume that there are "natural" explanations and that one need not postulate special intervention of divine powers. At the present state of our psychological knowledge, it is, I think, clear enough that the mystical interlude is the result of some special and unusual process that goes on within the human personality and need not require any external *special* divine intervention.

It seems to me that the basic weaknesses of the psychological explanations described in Chapter Three are that they assume without actually saying it that the mystic is a rare person and that the mystical episode is, statistically at least, and aberrant form of human behavior. Surely, however, if they were Oriental psychologists, they would not make such an assumption, for the mystical interlude is the goal of much Oriental religious activity, indeed the only goal deemed worthwhile in many Oriental religious forms. In other words, the mystical experience, while it may not be exactly commonplace in the East, is at least taken for granted as being available to anyone who wants to strive for it.

Maslow suggests that peak-experiences may be universal, or nearly so. Lieberman's research indicates that as many as half of his respondents had had an ecstatic interlude; and the preliminary work of McCready and myself would suggest that as much as one-fifth of the population has frequent mystical experiences. We are therefore dealing with something that is not all that rare or extraordinary. We are attempting to cope with something that is fairly commonplace in the human condition, and in many parts of the world is almost taken for granted. That it is viewed as extraordinary, esoteric, bizarre, and perhaps psychotic in the North Atlantic elite culture may only be evidence of how far that culture has drifted away from understanding the basic elements of the human condition. I shall argue in this chapter that ecstasy is a form of human knowledge, knowledge, indeed, of the outside world and not merely, as the psychologists quoted in the previous chapter suggest, knowledge of one's own consciousness, much less some kind of "jammed up" computer program. Like all other forms of human knowledge, the ecstatic experience is a means whereby man understands the world of which he is a part, but it differs in being a more direct, immediate, and intuitive form of knowledge. The rapture that results from this intimate and direct experience is an analogue of the satisfaction that comes from solving a complex intellectual problem or the enjoyment that comes from reading or writing a great poem or listening to a great symphony. Mind you, I am not saying that mystical rapture is the same thing as pleasure at solving a problem or writing a poem; I am asserting merely that mystical rapture bears the same relationship to the form of knowledge which produced it as satisfaction over a problem solved bears to the form of knowledge which produced *it*. Every form of human knowledge has its own joys of fulfillment and satisfaction. Mystical rapture is merely the joy that comes from this particular form of contact with Reality.

The great heresy of the contemporary Western world is that the only kind of knowledge that is to be taken seriously and trusted is discursive, cognitive knowledge, that which is acquired by man's practical or technical reason. Concomitant with this are the assertions that the only kind of truth is that which can be empirically verified, and the only kind of language fit for human communication that of logically validated prose. In other words, that knowledge and language which is appropriate for discourse in the empirical sciences is the only one that is really worth developing in man, because it is the only one that can have any demonstrable validity.

The proposition as stated that baldly would be objected to by many people. However, one need only read the writings of the logical positivists and those who have been influenced by them to realize that a good number of very intelligent men are willing to rule out the mythopoetic, the metaphysical, and of course the mystical as valid human forms of knowledge.

But even those of us who may disagree with the positivists in theory have been tremendously influenced by them in fact. Professor Timothy Healy, the Vice-Chancellor of City University of New York, told me once that the black students in his freshman seventeenth-century English poetry course had a much better ear for and capacity to create poetry than did the white students. Knowing that Father Healy was not the sort of man to repeat hoary racist stereotypes about natural rhythm, I asked how that could be. "Easy," he said with his characteristic wink. "We're all born poets, and we have to learn to speak prose. Every child comes to school a natural poet, and our school system proceeds to make every effort possible to destroy his poetic capabilities and to turn him into an incorrigible prosist. Schools are so bad in the neighborhoods where the black kids come from that they manage to escape twelve years of education with their poetic instincts barely impaired."

If our mythopoetic capacities are systematically drummed out of us by our schools—and probably by the mass media too—there is all the more reason to assume that pragmatic, technological Western education leaves little room for the continuation of the exercise of mystical capabilities. Furthermore, since it is certainly true that mystical capability can only be exercised when one is reasonably free from distraction, the noisy environment in which young people grow up drowns out their mystical abilities. The sight and sound of the TV tube leaves little time for the solitude that is an absolute prerequisite for mystical development. What is surprising about contemporary North Atlantic culture is not that there is less mysticism than allegedly exists in the East but that there are as many people who experience mystical interludes as apparently do. The 20 percent of the American population that reports frequent ecstatic experiences does so despite immense obstacles. In a culture without silence, where only technical reason is valued, where the educational system conspires to turn everyone into a prosist, and where the mystical interlude is equated with mental illness, it is not easy to be an ecstatic. In fact it is so difficult that many people would never admit to having ecstatic experiences and would never dream of describing themselves as "ecstatics."

Some critics of Abraham Maslow, and some of those who haven't read Marghanita Laski or heard of Lieberman's research, or McCready's and mine, remain profoundly skeptical. How, they argue, can a phenomenon be so widespread and yet so unknown to most serious researchers? Rather than believe that social science research has overlooked completely, or almost completely, an extraordinarily important dimension of the human condition, these scholars are ready to deny the evidence of empirical data which their own scientific world view ought to consider sacred.

I am reminded of the story of the mental patient who insisted to his psychiatrist that he was dead. The psychiatrist tried everything to persuade the patient that he was still alive. To no avail. The patient persisted in believing himself to be dead.

Finally, in desperation, the psychiatrist said, "Do dead men bleed?"

The patient thought for a while and said, "No, in no way do dead men bleed. Everybody knows that."

"Therefore," said the psychiatrist, "if you bleed, you're not dead."

"That's right," the patient assented.

The doctor produced a long needle and stuck it into his patient.

"Well, I'll be damned," the man said, "dead men do bleed."

An alternative explanation would be that the intellectual blinders of contemporary social science are such that so widespread and important a human phenomenon could be readily and completely ignored simply because the narrow perspective of social science said that it couldn't possibly be there. As I shall suggest in a later chapter, psychedelic culture is a response of some young people to American elite culture's refusal to consider other forms of knowledge besides the cognitive and the technical as either valid or desirable.

I would argue that there are at least four kinds of human knowledge.

The first would be the cognitive or rational or discursive, which furthers the work of science and technology and which (in the scientist's viewpoint) in its debased form of "common sense" governs most of the events of our everyday lives.

The second, metaphysical, which is a form of knowledge closely related to rational cognition, is concerned more with ultimate issues than the immediate data of sense experience. Metaphysical knowledge observes the conventions of discursive knowledge, the language of prose, the laws of logic, the methods of rational discourse. It differs from prose in its concern for the ultimate rather than the proximate.

The third form, mythopoetic knowledge, is also more concerned with the ultimate. It seeks to embody human experience in forms that appeal not only to the intellect but to the whole person. Hence in both its style and language it uses symbols rather than prose and strives to illumine the ambiguities of conditions and situations rather than to explain them. There is a strain toward concern for the ultimate in all mythopoetic insight and communication. Every poem, every novel, tries to say something basic about the human condition. Religion is that form of mythopoetic knowledge and discourse which is explicitly concerned with the ultimate. It purports to provide answers, not so much for the intellect as for the whole person, to the most basic and fundamental questions a human being can ask. The poet shares with the metaphysician a concern for the ultimate, but he also shares with the scientist a concern for the hard data of human experience. However, that data is expressed not in logical propositions or mathematical formulae but in pictures, images, rituals, stories, and symbols.

The fourth form of knowledge, the mystical, resembles the metaphysical in that it is concerned with the ultimate, is like the mythopoetic in that it does not deal with logical propositions or the laws of discursive reasoning, and is like science in that it comes into contact with the hard data of external reality. It is different, however, in a number of critically important ways. It is demonic (in Rollo May's sense) in that it takes possession of the whole personality far more than any other knowledge. It is immediate. One comes into contact with the real without the need for either prose or poetry; it requires neither logical proposition nor symbolic representation. The real is encountered directly and as it is. Furthermore, because this knowledge is direct and immediate and needs neither propositions nor images, it is possible for the Real to "rush in," without having to operate through any of the intermediary tools that other forms of knowledge must utilize—hence the passivity that characterizes virtually all mystics in the course of their experiences.

Mystical knowledge ("knowledge" may be a poor word, because it is identified so closely with discursive reasoning; "apprehension" may be better) cannot be expressed adequately in symbols because it is obtained without them—co-naturally, as it were, through the immediate union of the knowing subject and the object known.

Finally, mystical knowledge is inevitably religious even though the explicit content may have nothing to do with doctrinal propositions or with denominational affiliation. Even the unreligious mystic experiences a sense of The Way Things Are, which for a sociologist of religions like myself or a historian of religions like Mircea Eliade is precisely what religion is. The mystic, even the unreligious one, has had a vision of Ultimate Reality whether he thinks that Reality is personal or not. I would even go so far as to suggest that under normal circumstances—when the personality of the person experiencing the ecstasy is not predisposed to strong conviction or inclination to believe that life is absurd, capricious, or evil—the ecstatic experience reveals graciousness (either small or capital "G," as you please). Certainly Maslow's research indicates that virtually all peak-experiences are those of graciousness. In addition, recent research done on the psychodynamics of hopefulness and the universal mythology of the dream symbolism of death and rebirth indicates that a conviction of hopefulness is built into the structure of the human condition. If an unassailable conviction of graciousness is indeed part of the structure of the human condition, that conviction would necessarily come rushing to the surface precisely at the time when the person is in direct and immediate contact with the structure of existence itself.

But how does this immediate and direct contact with Reality, independent of symbols and propositions, occur? At this point in our knowledge of the subject, it is impossible to describe precisely and empirically just what the psychological and psychodynamic processes at work in the mystical experience are. As long as psychologists are content to compare it with pathological mental states we will never make much progress in acquiring empirically validated theories to explain (so far as social science can explain anything) the ecstatic experience. But then behaviorist psychology has not shown much interest in trying to analyze the mythopoetic creative process either, despite evidence which in other subjects would at least gain it a sympathetic hearing. They have also refused to take ESP seriously. Poetry is something that cannot be related to the nervous system, and therefore the behaviorist finds it of peripheral interest. Metaphysical discourse cannot be empirically validated, so it, too, is hardly worth studying as a psychological process. Everybody knows that ESP is impossible, so why attempt to devise and test theories that might explain why it takes place? If the human mind is seen as nothing more than a nervous system, then mysticism can be explained physiologically and nothing more need be said. With proper conditioning one can eliminate the phenomenon or, if the phenomenon is deemed desirable, one can reinforce it.

Psychoanalysis, which believes in the human unconscious, ought to be more open to the study of a form of knowledge that clearly calls into play the capacities Freud believed to be latent in the unconscious and the subconscious. But, caught in its own scientific and clinical presuppositions, orthodox psychoanalysis has been content with suggesting that the great mystics were in fact schizophrenics, working out the sexual frustrations of their childhoods in the erotic imagery they used to record their raptures. Both behaviorists and Freudians in effect put a label on the ecstatic experience which excuses them from investigating it further.

In the face of clear evidence that mystical knowledge and rapture are "boundary-breaking" experiences in which unity of the person and the cosmos is experienced, why do psychologists term it pathological and not "adult," since the blurring of the lines between self and Reality is a phenomenon of early childhood? Is such an assumption valid? Are there really sharp boundaries between the adult human person and the rest of reality, or are these boundaries artifacts of hypercultivated, hyperdiscursive technological man? If we pull back from our own presuppositions long enough to look at man in the world, it becomes clear that he is very much a part of the ongoing life processes of the cosmos. Rooted to the earth, he moves in an ocean of air; his life is sustained by biological and physiological cycles. His mood is affected by the weather and barometric pressures. Gravity, the rotation of the earth around the sun, the tilting of the earth on its axis—all of these may have a profound effect on his life. He is as immersed in the processes of the physical universe as any plant or animal. He is conscious of his own selfhood, which is distinct from other selves and in the ultimate sense uncommunicable to them. But the ineffability of that self does not mean that it has been separated from the rest of the cosmos. Every pore of his body, every nerve ending, is in deep physical contact with the universe. For example, the body is bombarded by the entire electromagnetic spectrum, of which only a tiny part is perceived by us as light. The infrared end of the electromagnetic spectrum gradually goes into lower-frequency light waves of radar, radio and TV, and radio beacons. At the ultraviolet end of the spectrum ultraviolet rays gradually become X-rays and gamma rays, as the wave frequencies become higher. As Buryl Payne points out in his *Getting*

*There without Drugs*,[1] electromagnetic waves vary in length from one-trillionth of a meter to one hundred meters, and all we perceive with our eyes is the tiny range between four-tenths and seven-ten-millionths of a meter; but we are bombarded by the entire electromagnetic spectrum. Similarly, we hear sounds ranging in frequency from sixteen to fifteen thousand cycles per second. Anything beyond that (and the sound spectrum goes to over one hundred thousand cycles per second—bats hear up to seventy thousand) is insensible to us. The mystical experience, of course, is not a gamma ray or a high-frequency sound, but we should note that we are immersed in a universe that is in direct physical contact with us, even if we are unconscious of that contact. The universe absorbs us even if we are unaware of it.

Every development of consciousness of self creates divisions between the person and the rest of reality that the infant does not perceive. But in the process of self-definition and self-individuation the growing person forgets that he is very much a part of the cosmos and all its processes. The person may be distinct from the rest of reality, but he is not discontinuous with it; there may be boundaries between self and world, but they are permeable and fuzzy. Modern man may have a more highly developed consciousness of self than did the Indian who lived "at one" with the primitive forest. He may know many things the Indian did not know, but the Indian was in touch with the world outside himself in a way that modern man cannot understand and indeed cannot even imagine. In this respect the Indian was superior to the modern, self-consciously alienated individualist. It should not be impossible to combine highly developed self-consciousness with a reverent attention to the life processes in which one is immersed. But it must be confessed that at this stage of evolution, the human race does not seem able to effect such a combination. René Descartes' mind machine still stares in self-conscious and haughty disdain at the mud, air, and water which constitute its physical being.

Thus I would submit that those psychologists who think that only in childhood are the boundaries between self and reality

[1] New York: Viking Press, 1973.

blurred have fallen victim to the same fallacy as those technologues who thought that to build an industrial society while ignoring the environmental and ecological processes was a form of human progress. Both groups assume that man is sharply distinct from the rest of reality—and then lament man's alienation. In fact, man is inextricably enmeshed in the universe. It is the beginning of wisdom to understand this fact; it is the beginning of mysticism to enjoy it.

In the mystical episode the person consciously experiences his intimacy with the cosmos. He becomes aware that he is caught up in the processes of the universe; he is in intimate contact with the world, the forces that underpin it, and with the basic life force of existence—whatever that force may be called. The mystical interlude is an experience of intimacy with the Ultimate. In fact, of course, we are at all times in physical contact with the cosmos; it impinges on us, absorbs us, permeates and pervades us every second of our existence, not only when we were children. The child may be more aware (scarcely reflectively so) of this fact. In the mystical interlude, the adult "remembers" his union with the cosmos once again and experiences it as occurring in the here and now. He also finds that union overwhelmingly good, true, and beautiful—so much so that he is "torn out" of ordinary life and bathed in fire and light. Under ordinary circumstances the cosmos, which he experiences as intimately present, and the life processes, which he physically feels surging through him, are understood as being incredibly gracious and benign.

But is there really an Ultimate, or Life Force, or Principle of Reality that underpins the processes of the universe? And is it available for immediate and direct contact to any conscious agent enmeshed in the forces of the universe? These are metaphysical and religious questions. At the metaphysical level one can say that the ecstatic experience is merely one of Being or Existence without having to postulate whether Being or Existence are either personal or transcendental. Indeed, in Eastern ecstatic experiences it would appear that the Being contacted is transcendental but not personal. Whether the Reality encountered in ecstasy is a personal Thou is a religious question. To analyze it in detail and assay an answer is beyond the scope of this book. It is sufficient to say, I think, that the

Christian and the Jew have always believed that Reality is a Thou, and that what is encountered in the ecstatic rapture is not merely a Life Force or an Ultimate Reality or the Ground of Being, but an Other.

However, one need not postulate an Other for my model of the ecstatic experience. It is sufficient to say that the mystic has had a direct and immediate contact—by a process which we do not yet understand—with the Fundamental Reality that operates within the physical properties of the universe in which he finds himself enmeshed. His co-natural knowledge is direct and immediate and absorbs the whole person, taking possession of the body and the spirit without the need of such intermediaries as propositions or symbols. In the ecstatic interlude the person does not so much admit into his being the forces which swirl around him and the Force which underpins them, he rather acknowledges their presence. We are already at one with the hydrogen-nitrogen-oxygen cycles, the processes of growth and decay, day and night, autumn and spring, sleep and waking, death and rebirth. In the ecstatic interlude we are taken possession of by that which we already possess.

The triggers of the ecstatic experience can be viewed as signals which remind the person of his co-naturality with the universe. A splendid crash of sound in a symphony, a rose-colored cloudbank hanging over a lake at sunset, the misty quiet of a stained-glass cathedral (in Paul Claudel's case, at the first vespers of Christmas), the stars set in the night-sky canopy, a particularly pleasurable experience of lovemaking—all of these remind the human that the universe of which he is a part is overwhelming, and in fact overwhelmingly gracious. Triggers sweep away the distractions, the troubles, the anxieties, even the activities of the rational world, and leave man temporarily passive in the grip of Being and hence predisposed to experience, albeit transiently, the power of Being revealed totally and directly.

Ascetical disciplines practiced in both the East and the West, including meditation, fasting, Yoga, repetition of phrases, concentration on the mandala, are all forms of tuning out distraction to concentrate on the forces and the Force which possess one as a being in the world. Such devices may or may not be a prelude to the ecstatic episode; they surely do not guarantee it. For reasons we do not understand, ecstatic knowledge and rapture are unpredictable. Sometimes ecstasy occurs wtih little preparation, at other times it will not occur despite the most rigorous and systematic preparatory acts.

It is also true that some people are much better at it than others. If my model is at all useful, it implies that every man has some kind of mystical capacity, but for reasons of heredity and environment these capacities are unevenly distributed in the population—as are capacities for science, metaphysics and poetry. Some people seem to be "natural" mystics, while others, like myself, I fear, are "naturally" very unmystical. How much of this may be the result of the physical arrangement of our brains and nervous systems, how much the result of childhood personality experiences, and how much the result of choices we have made in our life cycles are questions for which there are now simply no answers. Clearly, there are some people who are unmymstcial and others who can with some ease develop mystical capabilities with only a modest amount of effort. Finally, there are others—and these are probably the ones who have come down in history as the great ecstatics—who cannot help being mystical. The descriptions with which we began the book suggest that some have no choice but to be mystics. My hunch —based in part on our empirical data—is that there are many natural mystics in contemporary America, more than many people would be willing to admit. I think the young woman who expressed surprise that everyone didn't have "those kinds" of experiences was a natural mystic without even knowing it. If my hunch is correct, there is surely some poignancy in the fact that these people who have such capacities, which could mean extraordinary happiness to themselves and others, ignore or repress or minimize them because our society has told them for so long that they do not exist or are a form of mental derangement.

In my model, mysticism is neither to be condemned nor sought as a virtue. It is a given of our existence, and developing that capacity may result in virtuous activity and certainly an enriched and deepened personality. In a subsequent chapter I shall say something about how mystical and ecstatic experiences fit into Christian religious values. Suffice it to say for the present that unlike the a priori Oriental religions, the Yahwistic tradition has never considered mysticism to be the ultimate religious value.

To my Christian readers it may seem at first that my explanation of the ecstatic interlude does away with God. Teresa of Avila was a woman with either an extraordinary amount of natural ability at perceiving her intimacy with the life processes of the universe, or moderate mystical capacity who by a life of asceticism was able to tune out the distractions of ordinary time and place to put herself in frequent contact with the Life Force. I do not think Teresa experienced a personal deity who came down to take possession of her soul.

The God we experience in a mystical interlude is not one who descends from on high for a special event, but a God already present, immanent to us and to the world, which he supports in Being. God is not merely out beyond the universe; he is present in the sunset, in the foaming waves of the lake, the sexual organs of the lover. This is not pantheism (though the fear of it is so great in contemporary Catholicism that any suggestion of the immanence of God arouses fears of it) but traditional, orthodox Christian theology. God need not make any special intervention to become present in our lives, because in fact he is there all the time. The ecstatic interlude simply recognizes his presence. God is the Ground of Being, the Force which underpins the other forces, the Reality which is ultimate to all other realities.

The nonbeliever may well be prepared to concede the ecstatic experience as an intimate and immediate contact with the basic forces of the universe and even a basic Force. What he would deny is that the Immanent Reality he has encountered is also a transcendent reality. However, from the point of view of the Yahwistic religious tradition, there is no doubt that the Immanent Reality is also the transcendent Yahweh. The Yahwist differs from the nonbeliever in his definition of what it is that is encountered, not, I think, in the fact of the encounter.

I shall return in a later chapter to William James' discussion of whether mystical experience does indeed "prove" the immortality of the human person. At this point it is sufficient to raise one question in the dialogue between the Yahwistic mystic and the secular mystic. That question—whether the reality that is encountered in the peak-experience is both immanent and transcendent or only immanent—can be clarified if one asks what the Yahwistic tradition about the transcendence of God is designed to convey as an explanation of the meaning of the universe. Yahweh is not described as towering over all the other gods and transcending the universe that he has created merely because that is a nice way for God to be. The transcendence of Yahweh symbolizes the fact that the universe has a purpose beyond itself and that that purpose is supremely gracious. The reality of the universe as we experience it is a blend of absurdity and graciousness, with neither seeming to have ultimate domination over the other. Yahweh symbolizes the fact that in the long run graciousness does triumph over absurdity, love over hatred, goodness over evil. The transcendence of God in the Yahwistic symbol system serves principally to underwrite the Yahwistic conviction of the triumph of graciousness. So when the Yahwistic mystic asserts that that which he experienced as immanent in himself and the physical universe is also the God who transcends creation, he is merely asserting his belief in an ultimate graciousness which underwrites the triumph of good over evil and life over death—if not in this universe, at least somewhere, somehow, some way.

I would submit that the conviction occurring in most ecstatic experiences (according to Maslow, virtually all that he studied) of graciousness, of goodness, of unity, of love, of warmth describes precisely the same kind of universe that the Yahwistic symbol system describes. The person who has experienced a Maslowian peak-experience comes back to report that life is gracious. The transcendent Yahweh, huffing and puffing on Sinai, also asserts that life is gracious. I am not trying to "prove" the validity of the Yahwistic symbol system from ecstatic experiences. I am simply saying that it seems to me that there is a convergence between what the mystic reports about the reality he has encountered and what the twentieth chapter of the book of Exodus reports of the Hebrew religious experience in the Sinai desert, an experience about which all subsequent Jewish and Christian religious writing and preaching are but explication and commentary. The passionately loving God who announced on Sinai, uninvited and perhaps unwanted, "I am Yahweh your God" and "I am a passionate God" and "I want a faithful people" sounds very like the fiery, dazzling, loving, enraptured Reality that rushes in and takes possession of the human personality at the moment of ecstasy. Quite apart from my own personal religious faith, it does seem to me that the Sinai myth and all the Jewish and Christian symbols that have been developed to explain the notion of a passionately involved God, as well as the writings of mystics and ecstatics, are in fact describing a very similar if not identical religious experience—an experience of graciousness which quite literally boggles the human mind and overwhelms the human imagination. The point of doubt, I think, is not so much whether the mystic and the author of the book of Exodus are describing different or similar religious visions (the similarity is so striking, I think, as to be unquestioned); the real issue is whether we are willing to believe that the vision of graciousness accorded to the Hebrews at the foot of Sinai and to the mystic in his brief moment of rapture is really true. Is the world really that way? Does life really have that kind of meaning?

Finally, what can be said in terms of my model about drug-induced ecstasy? Minimally, one can say that ecstasy-producing drugs are the functional equivalents of the natural triggers or the ascetical practices which predispose a person toward an ecstatic interlude. The drugs either clear away the distractions of ordinary life by helping or forcing us to "tune out," or they reveal to us beauties, goodness, and truths of the universe to which we had only dimly paid attention before. The drugs may or may not produce ecstasy; they certainly produce heightened consciousness, and that in its turn may or may not lead to ecstatic rapture. If one reads what those who have experimented with drug-induced ecstasy write, it seems reasonably clear that "turning off" or, to use the phrase current among young people, "getting stoned," is by no means an automatic guarantee of rapture.

Must more be said? Is there a possibility that certain kinds of chemicals produce certain biological actions and reactions which not only predispose one toward ecstasy but actually activate those mysterious capabilities of our personality that become operative in ecstatic knowledge? Do the drugs induce the ecstatic insight itself? I do not think we know enough to answer this question, but I think we know enough to be skeptical of drug-induced ecstasy. It is unlikely that young people can be dissuaded from experimenting with hallucinogenic drugs even by research evidence that such drugs are physically and psychologically dangerous. It may well be possible that the human race is capable of developing a chemical agent that is harmless and will guarantee either the predisposition toward ecstasy or the experience itself. I think we will have to know a lot more about the ecstatic process itself to feel secure with drug-induced ecstasy. At the present time, in my judgment, it should be reserved for serious scholarly experimentation. Those using drugs to resolve religious or personal problems should know that they are taking serious risks and would be better advised to concentrate on the ascetical practices of the Orient if they feel the need for ecstatic experience. Certainly anyone reading Maslow would find the experience very attractive (and most college-age young people read Maslow). However, a troubled young person seeking help with drugs is not likely to be patient with the discipline required for the ascetical path to ecstasy. Perhaps such persons will grow up to understand that one really has to pay a price for anything worthwhile.

But what about the natural mystics? It does not seem fair that some people should have the capacity for Maslow's peak-experiences without having had to make any effort to acquire ascetical skills. As the late President Kennedy remarked, however, "Whoever said that life is fair?"

I have known two people who have extraordinarily well developed capacities for mystical insight. They are both remarkable people; I am dazzled by how much they know about The Way Things Are. They are—and it is hard to find the right word—"haunted." There is something, or Someone, on their minds. Their lives have higher peaks than mine, but also deeper valleys. I don't exactly climb up Mt. Carmel, but neither do I descend into the dark night of the soul. The great mystical writers of the Christian tradition made it quite clear that there are alternations between ecstasy and inner despair when one gets into a love affair with Being itself. I do not pretend to understand what the dark night of the soul is, and

I see no point in a book of this scope in trying to wrestle with the dark night aspect of mysticism. Suffice it to say that at least for the mystics I know, romance with the Ultimate is like all romance— if the "ups" are splendid and spectacular, the "downs" are awesome and terrifying. The person who wonders if he might experiment with a peak-experience should not deceive himself about what he is getting into. It can by its very nature be one hell of an experience.

# CHAPTER SIX

# Mysticism and Madness

All knowledge has its delights, but those of mystical knowledge are so powerful and so overwhelming that they literally "snatch" the person out of ordinary consciousness. He "sees" something; he understands something that is so extraordinary, so unspeakably beautiful that he is transported, or so it seems, outside of himself. Certain preconscious capabilities of his personality are restlessly forming and reforming patterns quite indifferent to the responses of the conscious mind to outside stimuli. Suddenly it "grasps" Something out there, and in that process a pattern is formed that seizes the personality. The union between object known and subject knowing may begin with the tentative initiatives of the subject, but once the contact has been established, the object takes over and, as it were, rushes in to transform the knowing subject. But what is it precisely that is known?

Virtually all the literature on mysticism points out that the mystic perceives the unity of the universe. He knows that All Things are One. It is a special kind of unity, unity in which things are bound together with a power and a force and an emotional strength that can only be described as love. The unity the mystic grasps in his interlude of insight is best compared with the powerful, compassionate, absorbing unity of human love. Indeed, whatever it is Out There that the mystic *sees* convinces him that it is the model of human love, which is but a pale reflection of it. Let us listen to what some of the mystics say. An anonymous medieval poet has God speaking to the soul with these words:

> I am true love that false was never;
> My sister, man's soul, I loved her thus;
> Because I would in no wise dissever,
> I left my kingdom glorious;
> I provided for her a place full precious;
> She fled, I followed, I loved her so;
> That I suffered these pains most piteous
> *Quia amore langueo.*[1]

Many of the mystics, particularly the Christian ones, have compared the experience of love and the mystic episode to marriage. John Ruysbroeck gives the following description in his Adornment of the Spiritual Marriage:

When we have thus become seeing we can behold in joy the coming of the eternal Bridegroom. . . . And the coming of the Bridegroom is so swift that he is perpetually coming and dwelling within with unfathomable riches; and ever coming anew in His Person, without interception, with such new brightness that it seems as though He had never come before. For His coming consists beyond time, in an eternal Now, which is ever received

---

[1] Happold, *op. cit.*, p. 41. "Quia Amore Langueo," from *Medieval Latin Lyrics*, trans. by Helen Waddell. New York: Barnes & Noble Books, division of Harper & Row Publishers, Inc. Reprinted by permission of Barnes & Noble and Constable & Co. Ltd.

with new longings and new joy. Behold, the delight and the joy which this Bridegroom brings with Him in his coming are boundless and without measure, for they are Himself.[2]

And the poet Shelley, scarcely an ascetic like Ruysbroeck, says much the same thing:

> That Light whose smile kindles the Universe.
> That Beauty in which all things work and move,
> That Benediction which the eclipsing Curse
> Of birth can quench not, that sustaining Love
> Which through the web of being blindly wove
> By man and beast and earth and air and sea,
> Burns bright or dim, as each are mirrors of
> The fire for which all thirst. . . .[3]

In the whole of Western thinking no more poignant description of the love encountered in the mystic experience can be found than that of St. Augustine in the tenth chapter of his *Confessions*:

> Too late loved I Thee, O Thou Beauty of ancient days, yet ever new! Too late I loved Thee! And behold, Thou wert within, and I abroad, and there I searched for Thee; deformed I, plunging amid those fair forms, which Thou hadst made. Thou wert with me, but I was not with Thee. Things held me far from Thee, which, unless they were in Thee, were not at all. Thou calledst, and shoutedst, and burstest my deafness. Thou flashedst, shonest, and scatteredst my blindness. Thou breathedst odours and I drew in breath and pant for Thee. I tasted, and hunger and thirst. Thou touchedst me, and I burned for Thy peace.[4]

Augustine's medieval successor, Bernard of Clairvaux, echoes the theme of marriage in clearly erotic language:

> Rightly, then, does the bride renounce all other affections and give herself up wholly to love and to love alone, for she is able to make some return to love by loving him back again. For when she has poured her

2 *Ibid.*, p. 89.
3 *Ibid.*, pp. 91–92.
4 Happold, *op. cit.*, p. 203.

whole self forth into love, how little this is when compared with that foun-
tain which flows in a never-failing stream! Truly they flow not in equal
volume, the Lover and love himself, the soul and the Word, the bride and
the Bridegroom, the Creator and the creature: it is as though we were to
compare a thirsty man with the spring he drinks from. Well then: shall
the prayer of the bride that is to be, the deep longing of her aspirations,
her loving fervour, her confident anticipation, come to nought and be
wholly cast away, on this account, that she cannot keep pace with this
Giant who runs ahead, that she cannot vie in sweetness with the honey,
in gentleness with the lamb, in whiteness with the lily, in clarity with the
sun, in charity with Him who is Himself Charity? No; for though the creature may love less than He, for that she is less, yet if she love with her
whole self, nought is wanting there where the whole is given. Wherefore, as
I have said, thus to love is to be joined together in wedlock, for it is impossible that a soul should love thus and not be beloved; and it is the unity of
their two wills that makes the complete and perfect marriage, to which
nothing is lacking.[5]

A couple of centuries after Bernard, Jami, a Sufi poet of Persia,
encountered the same lover:[6]

> The Loved One's rose-parterre I went to see,
> That beauty's Torch espied me, and, qouth He,
>    "I am the tree; these flowers My offshoots are.
> Let not these offshoots hide from thee the tree."
>
> What profit rosy cheeks, forms full of grace,
> And ringlets clustering round a lovely face?
>    When Beauty Absolute beams all around,
> Why linger finite beauties to embrace?

In the English mystical tradition, the unknown author of the
manuscript of *The Cloud of Unknowing* also describes the dart of
longing love that he experienced:

And therefore I would leave all that thing that I can think, and choose
to my love that thing that I cannot think. For why; He may well be loved,
but not thought. By love may He be gotten and holden; but by thought

5 Happold, *op. cit.*, pp. 205–6.
6 *Ibid.*, p. 211. Trans. by E. H. Whinfield.

never. And therefore, although it be good sometime to think of the kindness and the worthiness of God in special, and although it be a light and a part of contemplation: nevertheless yet in this work it shall be cast down and covered with a cloud of forgetting. And thou shalt step above it stalwartly, but listily, with a devout and a pleasing stirring of love, and try for to pierce that darkness above thee. And smite upon that thick cloud of unknowing with a sharp dart of longing love; and go not thence for anything that befalleth.[7]

Dame Julian of Norwich, a friend of Richard Rolle, also describes a pervasive and powerful love:

And from that time that it was shewed I desired oftentimes to learn what was our Lord's meaning. And fifteen years after, and more, I was answered in ghostly understanding, saying thus: Wouldst thou learn thy Lord's meaning in this thing? Learn it well: Love was His meaning. Who shewed it thee? Love. What shewed He thee? Love. Wherefore shewed it He? For Love. Hold thee therein and thou shalt learn and know more in the same. But thou shalt never know nor learn therein other thing without end. Thus was I learned that Love was our Lord's meaning.

And I saw full surely that ere God made us He loved us; which love was never slacked, nor ever shall be. And in this love He hath done all His works; and in this love He hath made all things profitable to us; and in this love our life is everlasting. In our making we had beginning; but the love wherein He made us was in Him from without beginning: in which love we have our beginning. And all this shall we see in God, without end.[8]

John of the Cross also speaks of the spiritual betrothal:

By this spiritual flight which we have just described is denoted a lofty estate and union of love wherein after much spiritual exercise God is wont to place the soul, which is called spiritual betrothal with the Word, the Son of God. And at the beginning, when this is done for the first time, God communicates to the soul great things concerning Himself, beautifying it with greatness and majesty, decking it with gifts and virtues, and clothing it with knowledge and honour of God, just as if it were a bride on the day of her betrothal. And upon this happy day, not only is there an

[7] *Ibid.*, p. 277.
[8] Happold, p. 301.

end of the soul's former vehement yearnings and plaints of love, but, being adorned with the good things which I am describing, she enters into an estate of peace and delight and sweetness of love wherein she does naught else but relate and sing the wonders of her Beloved, which she knows and enjoys in Him, by means of the aforementioned union of the betrothal.[9]

And finally, Gerard Manley Hopkins in his poem "God's Grandeur" records a vision of love at work in the world that almost surely came from one of his own mystic experiences.

The world is charged with the grandeur of God.
It will flame out, like shining from shook foil;
It gathers to a greatness, like the ooze of oil
Crushed. Why do men then now not reck his rod?
Generations have trod, have trod, have trod;
And all is seared with trade; bleared, smeared with toil;
And wears man's smudge and shares man's smell: the soil
Is bare now, nor can foot feel, being shod.

And for all this, nature is never spent;
There lives the dearest freshness deep down things;
And though the last lights off the black West went
Oh, morning, at the brown brink eastward, springs—
Because the Holy Ghost over the bent
World broods with warm breast and with ah! bright wings.[10]

I will admit that my own tendency was to dismiss the language of mysticism as high-flown rhetoric, a rhetoric that became dull with constant repetition. "Love is fine," I said to myself, "but that seems to be all those people can talk about." It was only when I met some real, live mystics and became convinced that we must take them seriously indeed and listen quite carefully to what they say that I came to understand that their rhetoric was not an exaggeration but rather an understatement of what they had experienced. If one rereads the above quotations in the realization that

---

[9] *Ibid.*, p. 333.

[10] *Immortal Poems of the English Language*, edited by Oscar Williams. New York: Pocket Books, Inc., 1952, p. 458. Reprinted by permission of the Oxford University Press by arrangement with the Society of Jesus.

all the authors would themselves have been dissatisfied with all the dazzling praises they sang of the love that they encountered and that binds the universe together, as being understated descriptions, the phenomenon must have been awesome indeed. Whether the love the mystics report is really Out There or not may be a matter for some debate. But we must consider the possibility that they are right, and that there really is such Love abroad in the universe.

The scientific psychologists of the sort I quoted in a previous chapter will quickly insist that the ecstatic testimony is no *evidence* that there is love like that Out There. William James is solidly in the scientific tradition when he gives an agnostic shrug of his shoulders in answer to the question of the existence of a reality that corresponds to that the mystics claim to have encountered.

From one point of view, of course, such a stance on the part of psychologists is correct. There is nothing in the skills of their discipline that enables them to accept as scientific evidence the testimony of those whose assertions cannot be subjected to empirical validation. Yet, to say that something cannot be empirically validated is not to say that it is not real, but merely that it cannot be empirically validated. In the agnostic shrug of the shoulders, typical of most of those who have studied mysticism since William James, there is an implicit denial of the possibility of a reality Out There of the sort the mystics claim to know. James, more sophisticated than most of his followers, is not all that sure.

But if one cannot expect psychologists to accept the testimony of mystics as "evidence," one could at least expect that they might give something more than passing and perfunctory consideration to the possibility that the mystics might be right, that there may indeed be love in the universe of the sort the mystics describe. Surely it would not be violating any canons of psychological responsibility to raise the question of what life would be like if one truly believed that the universe was permeated by such love. The more recent counterculture enthusiasts of mysticism are superior to their psychological predecessors in this respect at least: they are prepared to concede that love is at the core of the universe. For unless I mistake the message of the mystics, that is precisely what they are trying to tell us.

I somehow sense we may already know it. That "love makes the world go 'round" is a cliché, and that love is the most powerful experience of human life is obvious. In those periods when we are "in love" we perceive, dimly perhaps, the possibility that this powerful unifying emotion might be the very stuff out of which the universe is made. What most of us have at least occasionally suspected might be the nature of Reality, the mystic claims to have experienced directly. Love is the nature of the Real, and that is his knowledge. While we may describe him as "deautomatized" or "regressive" or "schizophrenic" or "in a trance," and while we can produce the same effects with hallucinogenic drugs, the question still remains: what if things are really that way?

The argument of this book has been that the mystical experience is a way of knowing. Ecstasy either is, or at least results from, knowledge. But it is worth asking whether the reverse might also be the case. Might all knowledge have about it a certain touch of mystical insight? Might certain forms of knowledge, especially the sort that give rise to profound religious conviction, represent a form of mystical intuition without the ecstatic kick? Is it possible that an act of faith calls into play the same dimensions of the personality that are activated in the ecstatic interlude? Does the ordinary believer see the same thing the ecstatic sees, though perhaps less clearly? Or, to put it the other way around, does the ecstatic see the same thing the believer does but much more dramatically and immediately? Both leap beyond discursive reasoning; both perceive love at work in the universe; both have confidence in peace and joy as the result of their insight; the convictions of both are totally inexplicable in the categories of positivist empiricism.

It would never have occurred to me that faith and the mystical experience might be closely related phenomena if a mystic had not raised the possibility of it in a conversation with me. "There are," he observed, "many different paths to the fundamental loving unity of the universe, and ecstasy is only one of them." If he is right—and I think he is—then we can see the ecstatic experience not as something totally and completely different from our ordinary, prosaic human experience, but as simply one end of a continuum that we might call nondiscursive insight into the nature of the Real.

I have argued throughout this book that mystics are not madmen, and that they ought not to be equated with schizophrenics or even neurotics. However, it is also clear that some mystics are badly disoriented personalities, and while mysticism is not necessarily the same thing as madness, an ecstatic episode can put some personalities over the brink of madness. All the mystics I have talked to will confess that there is a tremendous burden as well as tremendous joy in seeing things The Way They Are. The dark night of the soul results more than anything else from the inability of the mystic to sustain his vision and to live up to it. Quite apart from the desolation that follows when the vision is gone and the terror which often accompanies "the knocking at the door" when it is about to return, the ecstatic episode still appears to be difficult to absorb and to integrate with the personality. All the mystics I know are healthy and happy people, but they have personal problems and minor neuroses like everyone else. They will confess that it is occasionaly difficult to combine a grip on the everyday world with the dazzling experiences they have had. It is reasonable to assume that in a normally functioning personality, an ecstatic interlude, while it may be temporarily disorienting, probably has a positive function for emotional development. This certainly seems to be true of the mystics with whom I have had an opportunity to talk. On the other hand, if a personality is not reasonably healthy, a mystical experience may be enough to unhinge it completely. Here, again, the analogue of the creative experience is helpful. Not all artists are lunatics; but clearly some of them are. Poor Vincent Van Gogh was a sincere, pious, well-meaning but unbalanced genius. If he did not have that splendid vision of color with which he was obsessed, he could have led, one presumes, an ordinary and only moderately neurotic life. But he simply could not cope with the awesome array of colors in which he was enveloped. His creative talents were too much for his fragile personality to withstand, and the result was madness—dazzling, brilliant, and productive madness perhaps, but madness nevertheless. Similarly, for a personality that is weak or badly integrated or incapable of coping with stress, mystical knowledge may be far too much.

There are certain kinds of neuroses (particularly the obsessive-compulsive ones) that exclude the possibility of mystical experience; but there are other kinds that surely do not inhibit mystical interludes and may even predispose persons to them. For such persons the clarity of vision of a mystical insight may indeed push them over the brink into schizophrenia, but it does not follow that mysticism and schizophrenia are the same thing.

Not all experiences of love are necessarily positive or healthy. Some people are terrified by love; others turn hateful and punitive when love seems to strip away their defenses; still others flee from it lest they be trapped. Some people are driven to wild trips of egoism by love, and others withdraw completely from all relationships so delighted by and hoarding of the experience of love. If love is such a multivalent phenomenon when the object loved is of the same order of being as the lover, the possibilities for strange behavior are multiplied many times when it is a cosmic loving force that one feels one is possessing and being possessed by. Those who have undergone frequent mystic states will ruefully admit that they are a mixed blessing. For those who are trapped between strong mystic sensitivities on the one hand and a weak personality structure on the other, such experiences can be a curse, a curse that gives the lie to the love encountered. What sort of love is it that drives the beloved to madness? The question is a fair one.

Mysticism is knowledge; it is an act of knowing by which a person breaks through to what he thinks is the basic structure of the universe. He discovers within that structure not merely unity but a unity of passionate love. We have no way of validating his insight empirically. Ultimate visions of Reality, whatever their content, are simply beyond validation. The mystic cannot prove to us that the universe is really passionate love, but neither can his critics prove to him that it is random absurdity, a meaningless interlude between two oblivions. That Love is Out There is an arguable position; the mystic who purports to be able to describe the Ultimate may be right or may be wrong—but *he may be right*.

Whichever he is, he is not a madman. He has an intuitive insight based on certain phenomena he has experienced, which phenomena have led others to similar conclusions without the raptures of delight and ecstatic overtones that the mystic has enjoyed. But the overtones and raptures can be dangerous to a weak or poorly structured personality. Whether a mystical interlude promotes personality development in a reasonably well-balanced personality is probably an appropriate subject for further research, though Abraham Maslow didn't doubt it. I shall confess that my own initial skepticism about mysticism was pretty well dissipated when I met a number of people who were clearly mystic and also clearly extraordinary human beings. I would not say that I would wish to be one; it is ultimately a gift, and my own prosaic gift functions well enough without the turbulence of ecstasy and rapture.

The sociologist is not a specialist in the modes of human perception. He must choose to believe those who say that mystical knowledge is possible or those who say it is not. If he chooses to take the mystics seriously, then he can proceed to investigate the structural and cultural correlates of ecstatic experience. The sociologist can assume that it is possible for humans to have a capacity for intuitive, co-natural contact with the world in which they are immersed without needing the intermediaries of symbols or propositions. The sociologist can further assume that thus far perceptual psychology has been either unwilling or unable to discover very much about how this particular kind of co-natural knowing takes place. He can assume that, like all other human capabilities, this particular one is unevenly distributed in the population. Many humans have virtually no capacity for mystical knowledge. In others the capacity is so strong that it seems to dominate their lives, and in yet others the capacity is actualized occasionally, frequently, or only once or twice. Finally, the sociologist can assume until the contrary is proven that the mystics are sensible, rational people who are not mentally ill and who are describing as best they can something they have really experienced. With these assumptions the sociologist can proceed to investigate the prevalence, the correlates, and the consequences of ecstatic experience in contemporary society. He would stress, I think, a study of the "natural" mystics, those who have had mystical interludes without the assistance of drugs or without any kind of deliberate preparation at all.

William McCready and I are presently engaged in a project that reflects the foregoing perspective. We noted first that in our own immediate network of relationships we knew three mystics. One of them had frequent experiences, though apparently at a fairly low level of intensity; another had had only one experience, which was extraordinarily intense and profoundly affected the course of her life; the third had apparently frequent and intense experiences. We hasten to add that all three are healthy, normally functioning individuals, living "ordinary" middle-class lives. They may be a bit happier and more creative than others of their age and social class, but one would have to know the three of them quite well to perceive anything different or unusual about them. Finally, when one does discover that they are different, they are not perceived as less attractive but rather more so. In each of the three cases the person did not raise the question of his (or her) mystical experiences but was ready enough to talk about it when we did. In two of the three cases the respondents had read none of the literature on ecstasy and were not even sure that the experiences they had could be described as ecstatic, much less mystical; but mystical they surely were, even to the extent of being accompanied by the traditional rose-colored or blue-colored hazy light.

Building on the work of previous researchers, we will document how widespread and how frequent ecstatic experiences are and what different varieties there are of them. The data reported by Bourque and Back would indicate that mysticism is becoming more prevalent, perhaps as a concomitant of greater social acceptance. Perhaps we will measure the willingness or the facility of the respondent to report ecstasy. Bourque and Back report an interesting finding relating to the ability of some people to tell others about what they have experienced.[11]

They hypothesize that there are at least two varieties of ecstatic experience, the religious and the aesthetic. In one report they document that 47 percent of their sample answered the aesthetic question affirmatively, 32 percent answered the religious question affirmatively, and 22 percent answered them both affirmatively.[12] They

[11] L. B. Bourque and K. W. Back, "Language, Society, and Subjective Experience," *Sociometry*, XXXIV, No. 1 (1971), pp. 1–21.

[12] L. B. Bourque and K. W. Back, "Social Correlates of Transcendental Experiences," *Sociological Analysis*, XXX (Fall, 1969), pp. 151–63.

further hypothesize that the difference between these respondents is the language they have available to them for describing the experience. Most people referred to the aesthetic element; however, those who had both the aesthetic and religious categories available to them chose the religious. This led the researchers to conclude that the experiences were the same, the only difference being in the respondents and their abilities to describe what had happened.

To facilitate the use of these baselines and the replication of such measurements on different populations and at different times in the future, we are attaching as Appendix A a selection of some of the questions being used in our own national sample survey. Hopefully, some will be used by future researchers.

In particular, we wish to explore the so-called dark night aspects of repeated ecstatic experience. The habitual ecstatic has both higher peaks and lower depths of experience than seem to be "normal" in the human condition. John of the Cross did ascend Mt. Carmel indeed, but he also went down into the dark night. There is some evidence in Laski's research of experiences of "loneliness" or "deprivation." The mystical writers of the Christian tradition also frequently describe their desires to escape from the "romance" in which they are caught, and apparently there are times with the habitual ecstatic when the alternation between peaks and valleys becomes a heavy burden. The "dark night" phenomenon is almost universally ignored in the counterculture and the literature on mysticism. Yet the contemporary mystic poet quoted earlier resonates with the mystic tradition of the past when he describes the ambivalence and the reluctance of the mystic in his poem concluding with the line, "Goddamn it Lord, is it you again?"

The most obvious questions to ask concern the "background variables" of mystical experience.[13] What correlations, if any, exist

13 The authors of this essay are trained in the skills of survey research. Humanists, psychologists, psychiatrists, drug freaks, and yoga and Zen enthusiasts (to say nothing of ecstatics themselves) will no doubt be extremely skeptical of the possibility of studying ecstasy through the techniques of this primitive but stubborn discipline. We will, however, persist in both our primitiveness and stubbornness and contend that if one wants to know how many mystics there are in the American population and what the background correlates of mysticism are, the best way to begin is to conduct a national survey and ask people whether they have had mystical experiences or not.

between mysticism or various varieties of mystical experience on the one hand and religion, social class, education, age, occupation, ethnic background, region of the country on the other hand? Are there certain fundamental world views (or "interpretive schemes," to use Luckmann's words, or "cultural systems," to use Geertz's) that are more likely to predispose some people to mystical episodes? Are there experiences in childhood, adolescence, or young adulthood that facilitate or impede the development of mystical capabilities? In a study of Catholic priests in the United States conducted by the National Opinion Research Center it was discovered that there was a —.20 correlation between family tension during childhood and "religious" experience in adult life.[14] One might hypothesize that a relatively benign family environment encourages a kind of primordial and fundamental hopefulness or trust which in turn is both reinforced and represented in the almost incredible hopefulness which marks most if not all mystical interludes that are described in the literature.

One would also want to know not only the triggers of each interlude but also the social and cultural contexts. What are the situations which facilitate the operation of a mystical capacity and what are those that impede it? What are its special "functions" and what dysfunctions does it have? How does society "use" the mystic, and how does he "use" society?

I. M. Lewis addresses himself to these quintessentially sociological questions in his *Ecstatic Religion*.[15] His literary style, like that of many other British anthropologists, is charming and urbane but allusive and elliptical and very hard to understand if you haven't been trained in the same kinds of schools that trained him. After a careful reading of his book, one may conclude with its author that mysticism does indeed have certain functions and that these func-

---

[14] The elements which were defined as constituting a "religious experience" were:

An overwhelming feeling of being at one with God or Christ.

A sense of being in the presence of God.

A deep feeling of being personally loved by Christ here and now.

Source: *American Priests,* NORC Report, National Opinion Research Center at the University of Chicago (March, 1971).

[15] London: Penguin Books, 1971.

tions vary from society to society, but such a conclusion is limited in its capacity to further the sociological understanding of mysticism.

Of particular interest will be the question of the immediate personal context in which an ecstatic finds himself. Will his own interpersonal environment provide support, sympathy, reinforcement, and understanding or is it basically hostile and suspicious? It seems to us to be possible that the power of the ecstatic experience, as it has been described in the literature, is such that a person who has had a particularly intense ecstatic experience in an unsupportive and suspicious interpersonal context can have a severe and depressing reaction. If a person is told he's a "nut" or "crazy" for having such an interlude, could he not in fact become mentally disturbed within that context of conflict and judgment?

In one of the cases that came to our attention, a young woman who had had an extraordinarily intense mystical episode was saved from severe depression being brought on by extremely hostile reactions to her enthusiasm only by the intervention of a sensible, stolid husband whose religious upbringing and Jesuit secondary-school training had prepared him to take for granted the possibility of ecstatic phenomena. In a quite calm and matter-of-fact voice he observed, "Oh, sure, my wife is a mystic. I don't mind; it's a good thing. I just wish there was somebody to cook my supper until she calms down." This combination of acceptance on the one hand and firm grip on the reality of daily life on the other prevented his wife's experience from becoming a psychic disaster. Indeed, it enabled her to convert it into a positive growth-producing event in her life.

We must also examine the possibility that in the proper context and under the proper circumstances, ecstatic experiences can be extraordinarily functional for human personality development and mental health. In other words, we must take Maslow's hypotheses seriously and subject them to empirical test. With all pertinent background variables standardized, is the ecstatic less authoritarian, less racist, more trusting, more open, more "self-actualizing," more likely to report high psychological well-being, more tolerant of diversity, and perhaps even more inclined to loose rather than rigid sexual role definitions? Far from being "some kind of nut," it may be possible that the ecstatic is among the healthiest and most "normal" of humans. It may even be—as the religions of the East have insisted—that under some sets of circumstances ecstasy can be induced with the precise purpose of facilitating personality development.

We are not asserting that mystical ecstasy is necessarily a means toward mental health, as do those who are so enthusiastic about drug-induced mysticism. We merely say that it is a question that lends itself to research, and it is time to begin that research soberly and seriously with all the appropriate methodological skills and restrictions. The subject should not be left in the hands of the counterculture enthusiasts. The methodology by which such research can be carried out will differ according to the skills and the tastes of the researchers. Our own strategy involves three phases:

(1) At the present time we are collecting data in a national study of basic belief systems in the United States from a sample size of 1,500.[16] The questions listed in Appendix A have been asked of all respondents. We expect that at least two hundred persons will fall into the "mystic" category. A detailed analysis of the background variables and of the present attitude and behavior of this subsample will be undertaken.

(2) If we can persuade an appropriate funding agency that there is a correlation between ecstatic experience and positive psychological health—as Maslow argues—we will then undertake a massive national "screening" project to collect a sample of 1,000 respondents who have had mystical experiences. On the basis of the analysis to be undertaken in phase 1 (which will be in effect secondary analysis of data collected for another purpose), we will elaborate a detailed questionnaire to measure the background, personality, attitudes, and behavior of those being interviewed.

(3) Finally, a team of clinical psychologists will interview the subsample of 1,000 mystics (perhaps 200–250) who have been chosen either because of the frequency or the intensity of their ecstatic experiences or because the relationship between their mysticism and

[16] This study is being carried out at NORC under a grant from the Henry Luce Foundation. William McCready is the study director.

the development of their personalities seems to offer promise of extraordinarily valuable insights into the positive potential of the mystical experience.

There are obviously a number of serious objections to such a strategy. How dare we reduce the experiences of Meister Eckhardt, Francis of Assisi or Teilhard de Chardin to questions of positive mental health? Or of personality growth? Or success of human functioning? Is not the enterprise that we describe almost a caricature of social scientific behaviorism? Is it not ludicrous to think that questionnaires, IBM cards, and computer outputs can deal adequately with human experience of direct and immediate contact with the Really Real?

By definition the mystical experience is ineffable. Words are inadequate to deal with it. Even the most dazzling poetry is apparently incapable of conveying what it is like. Electronic impulses on computer tape are not meant to be adequate descriptions of an ecstatic interlude. All they are meant to be is a useful tool for trying to understand a little better some of the aspects of the ecstatic experience. A particular advantage of using a rather rigid behaviorist approach to the study of mysticism is that it meets the behaviorist skeptics on their own ground with their own techniques.

All this may be a wild pipe dream. We concede that there is a certain element of folly in pursuing the kind of enterprise on which we have embarked. However, we believe that it is only through such speculative and carefully delimited follies that new and important areas to social research can be opened. If no one engages in unusual or bizarre research enterprises, then nothing new or exciting will ever be done. The risk of failure is high; one would be much safer trying to develop a neat multiple regression model that explains social mobility. Many a successful academic career has been built on such research. A study of mysticism that ends up with no correlation over .1 bodes professional disaster.

Sociology has prided itself on its courage in studying social deviancy. Homosexuals, lesbians, transvestites, prostitutes, drug addicts, prison and asylum inmates have all been carefully, respectfully, and sympathetically studied. Heaven knows (one should excuse the expression), the ecstatic is a deviant in contemporary society. The rubric that allows us to view the psycho- or sociopath sympathetically and objectively ought to allow us to take the ecstatic seriously at his own word so that we can investigate the social, cultural, and structural contexts in which he finds himself. To do so might be to open a Pandora's box, but presumably that is what serious social research is supposed to do.[17]

[17] This is not a sociological monograph, so I shall not attempt to describe the analysis that McCready and I are now engaged in with any detail. My own feeling is that the purposes of promoting serious research on mysticism will be better served by introducing this material to a reading public of broad proportions. Sociologists tend not to take seriously things that are written so that nonsociologists can understand them.

# CHAPTER SEVEN

# Ecstasy through Sex

It is almost universally accepted that certain sorts of experiences "trigger" the ecstatic experience. These triggers weaken the generalized-reality orientation; they slow down and make the person more readily available for a special-reality orientation. They "deautomatize us," simultaneously taking our attention away from the phenomena of everyday life and suspending temporarily the ordinary structure of our perceptive and cognitive processes.

But at the same time these triggers also act as links between that fundamental and underlying reality of loving unity that the mystic claims to experience and the perceiving agent who does the experiencing. The ecstatic does not encounter the universe in a disembodied, abstract, idealized, theoretical form; rather he encounters it incarnate. He experiences it as being somewhere. The universe, so to speak, lurks everywhere; the structure of loving unity possessed and possessing is not a disembodied form, but is rather something he encounters in a material object. The object slows him down first, and claims his attention; then it grasps his attention to such an extent that his ordinary perceptions and cognitions fade temporarily. And finally the object, or the fundamental unity within the object, pours into his personality and takes possession of him.

In principle almost any object could trigger a mystical experience. It must first arrest the attention of the perceiver and then force him to concentrate on that which lies beneath its appearance. G. K. Chesterton used to experience mystical interludes when staring at a pocket knife or a street lamp, and it may well be that mystical experiences of most people who do not have the literary skills to tell the rest of us about them can be triggered by such prosaic objects.

However, it does seem that certain sorts of phenomena—nature, music, church, children—apparently have special powers to trigger mystical experience. The most interesting trigger is sexual lovemaking, interesting because there is virtually no mention of it in the literature of mysticism. But both Marghanita Laski's research and that of McCready and myself indicate that it is one of the most frequent triggers of a mystical interlude. Laski, as we noted before, speculates that believers might not experience sex as a trigger of ecstasy because their morality would not permit them to think that something as low and base as intercourse could produce something as elevated as a mystical experience. It may also be, of course, that believers would be less likely to report such a triggering event or even to admit to themselves that the experience triggered might be something profoundly religious. Surely there is something in the puritanism which has pervaded Christianity for many centuries that would incline the Christian to keep sex and religion as separate as he could—at least consciously.

It may be that the literature of the past does not record sex as a trigger because most of those who composed it were celibate. But it is worth noting that they did not hesitate to use erotic language to describe what happened in the mystical interlude. Those noncelibates who had mystical experiences may have been inhibited from suggesting that sex could trigger ecstasy because of the persistence of the Platonic notion that authentic religion involves breaking free of the controls of the body and could scarcely come from something so fundamentally earthly as intercourse. It is possible, then, that only in the post-Freudian age could sex be acknowledged as one of the major triggers of mystical experience. It is also possible that only in a post-Freudian age could substantial numbers of people even permit lovemaking to lead to ecstasy. But one should be skeptical about the latter possibility if only because the erotic language of mysticism makes it unlikely that the link between the two experiences was ever entirely unperceived.

In principle, however, it is not unreasonable to believe that under some circumstances sexual orgasm can trigger an ecstatic experience. Intercourse does deautomatize somewhat our ordinary reality orientation. It does take us out of ourselves; it is an experience of passionate unity; it is an attempt at sharing, a temporary immersion in fundamental life forces. While it is not the same kind of experience as mystical ecstasy—and both Laski's respondents and the ones I have interviewed emphasized this fact strongly—the two experiences are similar enough that it is not surprising that one could lead to the other.[1]

It is reasonable to presume that much depends on the kind of sex a person has experienced. If it is merely a quick and hasty tension release, one could hardly expect anything more to follow. If, on the other hand, an orgasm results from an act of passionate interpersonal love, then it can be reasonably expected that something else might occur. Routine, hasty, furtive, exploitative, anxious sex hardly predisposes a person for anything. The human personality incarnated in the human body is the most obvious and most beautiful manifestation of the structure of the universe. The complementary nature of the two sexes, different yet ordered for union, may be the most obvious and most powerful revelation of the raw

---

[1] If sex can lead to mystical ecstasy, one is forced to wonder whether ecstasy can lead to sex. Does a married ecstatic, for example, experience a heightened urge for the body of the spouse after the mystical interlude—if not immediately after it, then within a space of several hours? There is no evidence either way, as far as I know.

power that structures the universe. In the ancient nature religions the deity was frequently described as androgynous, a he-she (or, in these feminist times, a she-he). Two human bodies locked in intercourse were thought of as recapturing, however temporarily, the fundamental union between the masculine and the feminine in the Ultimate Reality. The outsider might say that such an androgynous conception of God is an example of humankind creating God in its own image and likeness. The believer, on the other hand, would respond that the union of masculine and feminine in human lovemaking is one of the revelatory experiences by which humankind discovers the nature of the Ultimate. Intercourse reflects the Ultimate, the believer would argue. The divorce between religion and sex, begun by Platonism and completed by Puritanism, is false to a more ancient religious tradition and also false to the genius of Christianity, whose sacred book is filled with marital imagery.

It may be debatable whether sex would be more of a trigger for mysticism today than ever before. Surely the emphasis on interpersonal fulfillment through sex might be thought to make for better sex, and better sex might make for more mystical ecstasy. However, it does not follow that simply because of the emphasis on the interpersonal dimensions of sex there is in fact any less of the tension-release approach to sex today than there was in the past. We may talk a better game, but we may not play it better. In any case, as hard as it is for the puritan Christian to accept it, one can, I think, conclude that if there were better sex one would have to expect, almost on a priori grounds, more mystical experiences. The suburban man and woman who practice yoga or engage in Zen contemplation or work at consciousness expansion ought to realize that all of these are triggers secondary to the one available to them in the marriage bed each night. However, sex is likely to trigger ecstasy only in such circumstances where it takes place in an ongoing relationship in which both partners are constantly opening up their personalities to each other. One can perceive the fundamental structure of the universe lurking in the body of the other, and in particular in that body's capacity to be linked with one's own only in the context of an expanding relationship and in the leisurely and ele-

gant giving and taking of bodies. Unfortunately, this is not the way
it usually happens.

Let us think of a suburban upper-middle-class married couple.
They have been married for ten years and have several children. It
is late in the evening, and they are watching television. (Johnny Carson?) The husband has had a frustrating day at his job, the wife an
intolerable day at home. He resents her lack of encouragment; she
resents his refusal to assume some responsibility for the children.
They both have developed a series of unwritten laws about the
things they will not discuss, the subtle punishments they can impose
on each other without retaliation, the protocols of avoidance by
which they manage not to get too close to one another. They have
each developed a long hidden agenda of hurts, frustrations, and dis-
contents. It is not a bad marriage, mind you; everybody thinks they
are happy, and at times they even think so themselves. They quarrel
rarely, and their friends marvel at how well they get along with
each other. Their relationship seems to be casual and relaxed and
only rarely indifferent. Yet they have a secret dread of the interlude
at the end of the day between the time they go to their bedroom
and the time they fall asleep. The unspoken frustrations and dis-
satisfactions of their relationship are focused and concentrated in
that period of time, and so they delay leaving the TV, hoping to
postpone the awkwardness of preparing for sleep, an awkwardness
that remains difficult no matter how routine it has become. Each
hopes the other will go to bed first so that the tension generated in
the bedroom just before the lights go out might be minimized.

Perhaps, as they watch Johnny Carson, one or the other of
them has decided that this will be the night when intercourse will
be attempted. This decision will more likely be the husband's if
only because he has both the advantage and risk of being culturally
expected to take the initiative. The invitation may be accepted or
rejected, one or the other may want to have "good" sex tonight, but
in any case there is no evidence of great passion or powerful love.
Eventually they go to the bedroom.

Nothing may happen; they may both fall asleep. An indifferent
offer may be indifferently accepted, or a naked back, the curve of a

neck, the slight flash of an eye may generate enough interest so that neither will resist the urge for union. And then that apparently relaxed and indifferent couple who had been watching Johnny Carson a few minutes ago suddenly and dramatically are transformed. For a few minutes they writhe in passionate movement; tension is released quickly, and the bodies fall apart, partially satisfied, perhaps, but scarcely content or exalted by the experience. At least there will be several more nights before they will have to worry about making love again. The structure of the universe has scarcely been revealed in such an episode. The wife may fall asleep wondering whether Women's Lib is right after all about ritualized rape, and the husband may fall asleep cursing himself for his own masculine inadequacies and failings. Such an encounter a prelude to mystical ecstasy? Hardly.

Yet one must say that things are the way they are between those two people because they have both chosen to keep them that way. Their relationship may be perfunctory and frustrating, but it is safe. There are no risks involved. The interpersonal relationship is mostly impersonal because that way there are no threats or dangers to the basic core of selfhood. One will not lose oneself in such an intimacy, and while the payoffs are minimal, so are the dangers. Indeed, no ecstasy is triggered, but who wants or needs that?

May not sex as a paradigm of ecstatic triggers tell us a good deal about why so many of us are so completely devoid of mystical sensibilities? May it not be that the passionately loving universe is Out There, trying constantly to seduce us with oceans and lakes, rivers and sunsets, concerti, stars, moon, sun, and southwest winds, snow and ice, tulips and roses, and green grass and the smell of a sizzling steak on a charcoal fire? But if the universe is unable to seduce us into looking beyond ourselves and our narrow, fearful, frightened, anxious, hedging, timid personalities by means of the body of one whom we purport to love, then how can it seduce us any other way? If we can keep at bay the person with whom we sleep at night, we ought to have no trouble keeping the rest of the universe at bay. Most of us are quite successful at doing just that.

What if the mystics are right? What if there is passionate love Out There that is trying desperately to get through to us? Why then are we afraid? Why then do we hide? Why do we ignore all its multitudinous seductions? Why are so very few of us unable to resist its enticements? Maybe the mystic is wrong. Maybe there is no passionate loving unity Out There. Maybe those of us who don't take risks, who protect our pathetic frightened little egos behind massive systems of defense mechanisms of graduated punishments for those who dare to get too close to us are right. Maybe we are playing it safe in a dangerous, capricious, ugly universe. Music, laughter, sunlight, lightning, the starry heavens, a beautiful body—maybe they are all tricks, cruel jokes and deceptions. In the final analysis, neither the cynic nor the ecstatic prevails; most of us try to hedge our bets by trying to live somewhere in between the two extremes. The knocking at our doors may be a loud pounding, and most of the time we hear nothing. When we do hear it, it sounds faint and hardly worth bothering with.

# CHAPTER EIGHT

# Ecstatic Politics

Most of today's "mystical revival" is apolitical. Those who are bent on the pursuit of ecstasy deliberately and consciously withdraw from direct involvement in the political process. Either political activity is irrelevant or society is so corrupt that political activity is a waste of time. Politics are then rejected either in principle or as the result of a radical critique of the possibility of action in a society as corrupt as ours. Timothy Leary's famous exhortation to "tune out and turn on" summarizes the feeling of most of those who are seeking mystical experience. Not all of them withdraw permanently from the ordinary political and social activities, but their mystical interests and pursuits are seen as unrelated to daily events. Many of the youthful university faculty in their thirties, who spent their formative years in the New Left decade, have given up on social reform and revolution and are now interested in developing a life-style in which they can earn a living from the square society and pursue their own interests and values on the fringes of that society. Not all of them, of course, turn to mysticism, but this attitude of straddling the square world and the counterculture world is wide-spread, and some of those who share those attitudes are what might be called "part-time mystics." The underlying ideology seems to suggest that mysticism, like related counterculture activities, is a form of behavior to which one turns when one has despaired of changing the rest of the world. The assumption is that one engages either in politics or in mysticism, but hardly in both.

This opposition of mysticism and politics is not a necessary one. Even the briefest perusal of the history of Christian mysticism makes this clear. However, for some reason the advocates of the "new mysticism" seem scarcely aware that there was any Christian mystical tradition, and some like Buryl Payne in his otherwise ad-mirable book, *Getting There without Drugs,* even suggest that Chris-tianity is without a mystical tradition save for the exception of a few extraordinary deviants.

It may well be that the combination of mysticism and politics is unique to the Yahwistic (Jewish and Christian) tradition. Since it is a tradition that believes in a God of history and an Ultimate Reality working out its plans not merely in cosmological processes but also in the processes of human interaction, it is very easy for that tradition to accept the notion that mysticism may be relevant to social and political affairs.

The most frequent form that political mysticism takes in the Christian tradition is that of millennialism—the belief that the thousand-year reign of Jesus and his saintly followers, mentioned in the Apocalypse, is about to begin. The related belief of the Jewish mystical tradition is the messianic one—the conviction that the mes-sianic age has begun or is about to begin. One can make a persua-sive case (beyond the scope of this book) that the millennialistic and messianic cults of Africa and Asia are fundamentally Christian in their origin. Thus the famous "cargo cults" of Melanesia, which believed that a vast supernatural cargo was about to be dumped from a heavenly bird (much as the American transports dropped quantities of goods during World War II), were generally begun by prophetic leaders who either were Christians or were influenced by them. I would make the stronger assertion that even the secular messianic world views (of which the most influential is Marxism) could only happen within the Western Christian intellectual tradition. Marx's view of the classless society comes close to being a mystical vision, if it isn't quite one.

Not all millennialistic leaders are mystics, and not all political mysticism assumes millennialistic form—though in the Christian tradition most of it takes at least salvationist form. Mystical politics generally promise some sort of salvation for those who join. Nevertheless, much if not most millennialism takes its origin from the insight of a prophetic leader, and millennialist cults are the ordinary form of mystical politics.

One of the interesting aspects of messianic cults is how they seem to appear repeatedly in certain regions: Thuringia in Germany, and the backlands of Brazil, for example, have seen repeated millennialistic outbursts, the former in the late Middle Ages and early Rennaissance, the latter in the nineteenth and twentieth centuries. Similarly, the Andalusian region in Spain was the home of first religious messianism and then the secular messianism of anarchism. Certain sections of northern Italy saw the Lazerettini religious movement in the nineteenth century, and in the twentieth century that same region became the stronghold of Communist partisans in World War II.

Under certain sets of circumstances, particularly in times of acute social disorganization, millennialistic leaders find a ready audience for mystical prophecy. Norman Cohn in his classic *The Pursuit of the Millennium*[1] shows how the social disorganization in central Europe during the declining years of the Middle Ages created an atmosphere of religious and intellectual ferment. Plague, population explosion, expansion of business and trade, the slow disintegration of the old ecclesiatical and political structure—all created a highly fluid situation even before the Reformation. Similarly, the cargo cults in Melanesia, the ghost dances among the

1 New York: Oxford University Press, 1970. © 1961, 1970 by Norman Cohn. Reprinted by permission of Oxford University Press, Inc.

Plains Indians, the present quasi-Christian messianic movement in Africa, and the revolutionary movement in the backwoods of Brazil, such as that led by Anthony la Counselor,[2] had their beginnings in times of social and cultural collapse. The millennialistic prophet sees a vision of the old virtues being restored in the beginning of a New Age; he promises stability and virtue in a time of confusion and corruption, and he promises it with absolute certainty. Small wonder that people rally to his cause.

It is but one step from seeing a vision of unity and love to reaching the conclusion that that unity and love ought to be realized in the everyday world. If the everyday world is disorganized and evil enough, one can take the next short step and conclude that indeed the unity and love one has perceived in a mystical interlude *will* be realized. And it is yet another short step to decide that if the world will not cooperate in the implementation of one's mystical vision, then one will rally a band of saints to impose that vision on the world whether it wants it or not. The mystical politician, particularly in the throes of a millennialistic or messianic vision, can be an extremely dangerous fellow—as can anyone who decides he should impose virtue on his fellow man. A mystic has certainty; he has *seen;* he knows beyond all doubt and beyond all question and beyond all reconsideration. He has seen with such clarity that it may become intolerable that others cannot see it too. If he has an unstable personality, if the social environment in which he lives is unstable, it becomes relatively easy for him to insist that the only reason others do not see things the way he does and act the way he acts is because they are corrupt and evil. They must be constrained to be virtuous, and if they still refuse, they must be eliminated.[3]

The political mystic is not necessarily an inept politician; on the contrary, Thomas Müntzer and Anthony la Counselor, for example, were extraordinarily adroit political maneuverers. They built their organizations as shrewdly as any Chicago ward committeeman would. Nor was their shrewdness hypocritical, though occa-

---

2 See Euclides Da Cunha, *Rebellion in the Backlands,* Samuel Putnam (trans.). Chicago: University of Chicago Press, 1944.

3 Usually a short-term policy. Power can seldom be sustained by such drastic methods. The mystic and his band of saints are eventually eliminated themselves.

sionally they could produce a mystical vision at most opportune times. The absolute and unshakable conviction that they knew what was going to happen gave them much flexibility in dealing with political contingencies. They could be extraordinarily flexible as to methods, but, unlike other politicians in consensual societies, the millennialistic mystic cannot afford for a moment to be flexible about his goals or his ultimate vision, because it is from his vision that he draws all his motivating force.

It may be possible for democratic politicians to be mystics. Perhaps Thomas More was one such. But the combination will work only when the person involved is sophisticated and self-possessed enough to know that his mystical vision and his political behavior operate on different levels of his being. If a political leader permits his insight into the unity of the universe to intermingle with policy decisions about the amorphous, pluralistic, unpredictable contingencies of daily politics, then there will be trouble—particularly from the political opposition.

Two fascinating books have been written about the political mysticism that appeared at the end of the Middle Ages: Norman Cohn's *The Pursuit of the Millennium* and Steven E. Ozment's *Mysticism and Dissent*.[4] Cohn traces the social and cultural disorganization that culminated in the Anabaptist outbreaks of the sixteenth century. Ozment traces the development of the ideas that underpinned the movements. Both books focus on the fascinating figure of Thomas Müntzer, the half-mad itinerant preacher, who never considered himself an Anabaptist but rallied one element of the Peasants' Revolt in the city of Muhlhausen, only to be routed and executed by the young military genius Phillip of Hesse in 1525.

Cohn also describes the theocracy established in the city of Münster a decade later by the Anabaptist militant John of Leyden. His rule was bloody, cruel, and oppressive, one in which every conceivable human atrocity was committed in the name of the Kingdom of God. There can be no doubt that both Thomas Müntzer and John of Leyden were mystics. There can be no doubt either that both of them were madmen. Finally there can be no doubt that

---

4 Cohn, *op. cit.;* Ozment, New Haven: Yale University Press, 1973.

they were extraordinarily adroit political leaders who pulled a rag-tag movement together into what was for a period of time an extremely effective political force. Cohn's graphic description of life in Münster during the theocracy suffices, I think, to establish its horror. In the following quotations from Cohn, Matthys is the older associate and teacher of John of Leyden (whose surname was Bockelson). Matthys was the prime instrument in the establishment of an absolute dictatorship at Münster, but he was killed shortly thereafter; his place was filled and enlarged by his disciple, Jan Bockelson. Knipperdollinck was a rich local merchant, devoted Anabaptist, and one of Bockelson's fathers-in-law.

The Anabaptists boasted of their innocence of book-learning and declared that it was the unlearned who had been chosen by God to redeem the world. When they sacked the cathedral they took particular delight in defiling, tearing up and burning the books and manuscripts of its old library. Finally, . . . Matthys banned all books save the Bible. All other works, even those in private ownership, had to be brought to the cathedral square and thrown upon a great bonfire. This act symbolised a complete break with the past, a total rejection above all of the intellectual legacy of earlier generations. In particular it deprived the inhabitants of Münster of all access to theological speculations from the Fathers onward and thereby assured the Anabaptist leaders of a monopoly in the interpretation of the Scriptures.[5]

Bockelson's first important act was—characteristically—at once a religious and a political one. Early in May he ran naked through the town in a frenzy and then fell into a silent ecstasy which lasted three days. When speech returned to him he called the population together and announced that God had revealed to him that the old constitution of the town, being the work of men, must be replaced by a new one which would be the work of God. The burgomasters and Council were deprived of their functions. In their place Bockelson set himself and—on the model of ancient Israel—twelve Elders. It is an indication of his political shrewdness that the Elders included some of the deposed councillors, representatives of the guilds, a member of the local aristocracy and some of the immigrants from the Netherlands. This new government was given authority in all matters, public and private, spiritual and material, and power of life and death over all inhabitants of the town. A new legal code was drawn up, aimed partly at

5 Norman Cohn, *op. cit.*, p. 267.

carrying still further the process of socialisation and partly at imposing a severely puritanical morality. A strict direction of labour was introduced. Artisans who were not conscripted for military service became public employees, working for the community as a whole without monetary reward —an arrangement which of course deprived the guilds of their traditional functions and quickly led to their disappearance. At the same time the new code made capital offences not only of murder and theft but also of lying, slander, avarice and quarrelling. But above all it was an absolutely authoritarian code; death was to be the punishment for every kind of insubordination—of the young against their parents, of a wife against her husband, of anyone against God and God's representatives, the government of Münster. These last provisions could not possibly have been literally enforced but did provide the prophet with an instrument of intimidation. To ensure that it should be an effective instrument Knipperdollinck was appointed executioner and given the Sword of Justice and an armed bodyguard.[6]

Like community of goods, polygamy met with resistance when it was first introduced. There was an armed rising during which Bockelson, Knipperdollinck and the preachers were thrown into prison; but the rebels, being only a small minority, were soon defeated and some fifty of them were put to death. During the following days others who ventured to criticise the new doctrine were also executed; and by August polygamy was established. Bockelson, who had left a wife in Leyden, began by marrying the beautiful young widow of Matthys, Diever or Divara, and before long he had a harem of fifteen wives. The preachers and then almost the whole male population followed his example and began to hunt for new wives. As for the women, though there were many who welcomed the institution of polygamy there were many others for whom it was a great tyranny. A law was made by which all women under a certain age had to marry, whether they wanted to or not. Since there were very few unmarried men this meant that almost all women were legally obliged to accept the role of second or third or fourth wife. Moreover since all marriages with the "godless" were declared invalid the wives of emigrants were forced to be unfaithful to their husbands. Refusal to comply with the new law was made a capital offense and some women were in fact executed. On the other hand many of the established wives at once began to quarrel with the strange women who had suddenly entered their households. This too was made a capital offense and resulted in more executions; but no amount of severity could enforce domestic harmony. In the end divorce had to be

6 *Ibid.*, pp. 268–69.

permitted and this in turn changed polygamy into something not very different from free love. The religious ceremony of marriage was dispensed with and marriages were contracted and dissolved with great facility.[7]

It was not as an ordinary king but as a Messiah of the Last Days that Bockelson imposed himself. In order to do so he invoked yet another divine revelation—in which he may or may not have believed—and in a manner even more dramatic than usual. At the beginning of September one Dusentschur, a goldsmith from a neighbouring town, set up as a new prophet. One day, in the main square, this man declared that the Heavenly Father had revealed to him that Bockelson was to be king of the whole world, holding dominion over all kings, princes and great ones of the earth. He was to inherit the sceptre and throne of his forefather David and was to keep them until God should reclaim the kingdom from him. Thereupon Dusentschur took the Sword of Justice from the Elders and presented it to Bockelson, anointed him and proclaimed him King of the New Jerusalem. Bockelson fell on his face and, protesting his unworthiness, called on the Father for guidance in his new task. Then he addressed the assembled populace, saying: "In like manner was David, a humble shepherd, anointed by the prophet, at God's command, as King of Israel. God often acts in this way; and whoever resists the will of God calls down God's wrath upon himself. Now I am given power over all nations of the earth, and the right to use the sword to the confusion of the wicked and in defence of the righteous. So let none in this town stain himself with crime or resist the will of God, or else he shall without delay be put to death with the sword." A murmur of protest rose from the crowd and Bockelson continued: "Shame on you, that you murmur against the ordinance of the Heavenly Father! Though you were all to join together to oppose me, I shall still reign, for the Father will have it so; and my kingdom which begins now shall endure and know no downfall!" After this the people dispersed in silence to their homes. For the next three days the preachers delivered one sermon after another, explaining that the Messiah foretold by the Prophets in the Old Testament was none other than Bockelson.[8]

Terror, long a familiar feature of life in the New Jerusalem, was intensified during Bockelson's reign. Within a few days of his proclamation of the monarchy Dusentschur proclaimed that it had been revealed to him that in future all who persisted in sinning against the recognised truth must be brought before the king and sentenced to death. They would be extirpated from the Chosen People, their very memory would be blotted out,

7 *Ibid.*, pp. 269–70.
8 *Ibid.*, pp. 271–72.

their souls would find no mercy beyond the grave. Within a couple of days executions began. The first victims were women: one was beheaded for denying her husband his marital rights, another for bigamy—for the practice of polygamy was of course entirely a male prerogative—and a third for insulting a preacher and mocking his doctrine. These sentences may have afforded the new king a sadistic gratification and they certainly served to reinforce the domination of the male over the female Saints. But the terror had wider purposes than these; it was above all a political weapon wielded by a foreign despot against the native population. Bockelson was careful to build up his bodyguard out of immigrants. These men, who either had no possessions or had left them to come to Münster, were Bockelson's creatures and stood or fell with him. So long as they served him they were secure in the enjoyment of enormous privileges. Clad in magnificent robes, they could lord it over the ill-clad citizens. They also knew that, if hunger came, they would be the last to suffer from it. One of the king's first acts was to requisition all riding horses and turn his bodyguard into a mounted squadron. This squadron drilled in public; and the populace was quick to recognise in it an armed force which could be employed against an internal enemy as well as against the enemy outside the walls.[9]

Eventually other rulers rallied to the support of the prince Bishop of Münster, and after a long siege accompanied by intense suffering and starvation within the city, the New Jerusalem fell and its king was tortured to death. An unbalanced but brilliant politician caught in a mystical vision can be just about the most dangerous person the world can imagine. One Hitler every century is more than enough.

The merit of Ozment's book is that he shows the intellectual and theological background of late medieval mysticism that provided the raw material for mystics like Müntzer and Bockelson. (Though, curiously enough, Ozment sees little connection between the mystical tradition he traces and the behavior of Bockelson, who is mentioned only once in a footnote.)

Late medieval theology, working in an atmosphere in which mysticism was both common and admired, developed a theory of the twofold communication between God and man. There was the

9 *Ibid.*, pp. 275–76.

*potentia ordinata,* which was the ordinary way that God dealt with humans through the doctrines and sacraments of the Church and through the structures of ecclesiastical authority. There was also, however, the *Potentia Dei absoluta,* the abstolute power of God, by which He could if He chose "communicate immediately with men, to speak more conclusively in the depths of the individual heart than through all the official writings and ceremonies of even the most holy institution. It offered its successful practitioners a certitude and perfection which a doubting and imperfect world does not even pretend to make possible." [10]

There was in the human personality a "spark" (*synteresis*) or a "ground of the soul" (*Seelengrund*), that is, an indestructible orientation to God through which God could communicate directly to the human person independent of the Church. This synteresis was a remnant of man's innocent perfection before original sin.

Bonaventure, a medieval theologian, as well as the German mystics Meister Eckhart and Johannes Tauler, believed absolutely in this spark of the soul. As Tauler put it:

The soul has a spark, a ground in itself, whose thirst God, even though he can do all things, cannot quench with anything except himself. He could give it the spirit of the forms of everything he has ever created in heaven and on earth, and it would still not be sufficient to satisfy it.[11]

There was a strong anti-intellectual and anti-institutional possibility in this doctrine of synteresis: mystical theology was not only the most perfect knowledge, it was also the knowledge in which "young girls and simpletons can excel." [12] In other words, if there is a special channel for God that does not depend on either human learning or institutions, then the individual person can dispense with both learning and institutions if he is able to actualize this communications channel. As Ozment points out, in this theory there was the raw material for immense ecclesiastical and political dissent.

10 Ozment, *op. cit.,* p. 2.

11 *Die Predigten Taulers,* Ferdinand Vetter, ed. Berlin: 1910, pp. 137. As quoted in Ozment, p. 7.

12 Jean Gerson, *De mystica theologia speculativea,* Cons. 30, 78.33–34. As quoted in Ozment, pp. 8–9.

Perhaps the most influential book in the translating of this potential into Lutheran and Anabaptist dissent was the *Theologica Deutsch*, a book by an unknown German author published by Martin Luther in 1516. To its readers it became clear that what the medieval theologians had considered exceptional—the communication of God to the individual through the synteresis—was no longer a rarely exercised option but the ordinary de facto form in which God communicated with humans. One did not need churches, one did not need kings or popes; one needed only the individual soul and God. As Valentine Weigel, a crypto-Anabaptist, remarked:

Man must bring forth sheer passivity, resignation, a surrendered will, a dying to self, and hold himself still. For as soon as man goes out of himself with his own will, just so soon does God enter with his will.[13]

Luther and his colleagues were fully prepared to shake the ecclesiastical order, but they were shocked and offended when others were willing to push such a theological mysticism to its logical conclusion. Despite Luther's criticism, Thomas Müntzer proclaimed the need for a cleansing slaughter since the political and ecclesiastical orders were corrupt beyond hope:

I tell you truly that the time has come for bloodshed (*ein Blutvergiessen*) to fall upon this impenitent world for its unbelief. . . . Why do you want to let yourselves be led around by your noses any longer? One knows full well and can prove it with Scripture that lords and princes as they now present themselves are not Christians. Your priests and monks pray to the Devil, and there are ever fewer Christians. All your preachers are hypocrites and worshipers of man. Why do you want to hope [in them] any longer?[14]

In other words, once you had established direct contact with God, political and religious intermediary institutions were no longer necessary. Indeed, the next step was to realize that it was God's will that these established orders were corrupt and ought to be destroyed. Müntzer did not begin the Peasants' Revolt, and indeed the segment

13 *Von der Bekehrung des Menschen,* pp. 18–19. As quoted in Ozment, p. 47.
14 Ozment, p. 78.

of it with which he became allied was somewhat on the fringes of the movement; but he certainly assumed leadership of those forces at Muhlhausen during its last days. The alliance was a natural one, for both the revolting peasants and Müntzer believed that they had a divine mandate to sweep away the established order. The mystical theology of Bonaventure, Eckhart, and Tauler had been converted into a political movement with revolutionary thrust; and that it was easily put down by that order does not negate the considerable cohesion and force generated by spiritual vision coupled with political deftness in a time of upheaval and uncertainty.

Norman Cohn's epitaph for Thomas Müntzer is an appropriate one:

> More curious is the resurrection and apotheosis which he has undergone during the past hundred years—Russian as well as German—Marxists have inflated Müntzer into a giant symbol, a prodigious hero in the history of the "class war." This is a naive view, and one which non-Marxist historians have countered easily enough by pointing to the essentially mystical nature of Müntzer's preoccupations, his general indifference to the material welfare of the poor. Yet it may be suggested that this point too can be over-emphasized. Müntzer was a *propheta* obsessed by eschatological phantasies which he attempted to translate into reality by exploiting social discontent. Perhaps after all it is a sound instinct that he has led Marxists to claim him for their own.[15]

Presumably the reader will not miss Professor Cohn's irony.

While much of the contemporary mystical revival seems quite apolitical and indeed seems to represent a withdrawal from the possibility of politics, it would be foolish to overlook the extraordinarily powerful political forces that may be latent in mystical experience. One could argue that, just as the end of the Middle Ages gave rise to mystical movements which later became violent political movements, so the end of the modern world might be creating a mysticism that in the not too distant future will assume political overtones. Tauler and Eckhart were not revolutionaries; neither was the author of the *Theologia Deutsch*. Martin Luther, who gave the book to the public, was scarcely a political revolutionary; he denounced

[15] Cohn, *op. cit.*, p. 271.

the Peasants' Revolt and the Anabaptist uprising and was completely identified with the secular princes' consolidation of power. Timothy Leary, Mike Murphy of Esalen, the devotees of Zen, Yoga, and Transcendental Meditation seem harmless enough, but somewhere—passing out literature on a street corner, or basking nude in the pool at Esalen, or smoking marijuana or dropping acid in a university neighborhood, or meditating in the desert near Taos—there is a potential visionary who is not content to withdraw from the square society but is bent on transforming it to accord with his vision. There are undoubtedly thousands of potential Bockelsons running loose in the country today; all we need is to have one of them turn out to be a political genius, and there will be trouble for the rest of us.

James Madison and the other men who put together our republic lived much closer to theocracies than we do. They constructed a constitutional order to prevent minorities from seizing and exercising power. American society is probably safe from a John of Leyden, but we would be ill advised to bet on it.

Most of the "ordinary" mystics, the unself-conscious ones, the ones who never go to Esalen and do not need drugs to produce ecstasy, are not inclined to withdraw from everyday social activities; nor are they motivated to direct the world toward their own visions. Some of them are involved in politics and social activism, but it is well contained within the limits of conventional conservative-liberal bounds. But in politics, as in everything else, a mystical vision can be a two-edged sword. It can illumine, create, and direct; but if it happens to the wrong person at the wrong time, it can be terribly destructive both for himself and for all around him.

In this chapter I have concentrated on the problem of the mystical visionary without political sense or skill. Sometimes, of course, it is hard to distinguish between the madman and the patriotic giant. Was the litle band of poets and mystics who seized the General Post Office in Dublin on Easter Monday, 1916, acting in the finest traditions of Brian Borou, Silken Thomas, and the Wexford revolutionaries of 1798? Or were they, as one native Dubliner suggested to me, nothing but a bunch of "Gombeen"? ("Phoney" would be a charitable English translation of the word.)

Hitler's vision of a thousand-year Reich was diabolic. Padraig Pierce's vision of Ireland, one and indivisible, was ambiguous. Gandhi's vision of a free nonviolent India seems to have been positive and constructive. Persistence, patience, endurance, dedication, confidence—these are all qualities of the mentally healthy mystic that will stand him in good stead if he happens to be a politician. Dag Hammarskjöld, for example, was both a mystic and a patient, skillful politician and diplomat.

It is possible, therefore, that ecstatic experience reinforces, deepens, and enriches a sensitive, subtle and sophisticated political commitment. It surely did in Hammarskjöld's case, and in Gandhi's, too. Perhaps it also did in the case of Martin Luther King. Still, society would be much better off if each prophet who came down the turnpike believing himself to be another King or Gandhi or Hammarskjöld could at least pause to consider the possibility that he might be a modern day John of Leyden.

And how can the rest of us tell the difference between a Hammarskjöld and a Leyden? In American society it is not very difficult. If you encounter an ecstatic politician, ask yourself how good he is at precinct work. In our country there is no substitute for precinct work, and a would-be political leader who thinks there is should be given a one-way ticket to the New Mexican desert.

# CHAPTER NINE

# Mysticism and Faddism

The reasons for today's revival of mysticism become clearer if we accept the proposition that the mystical is a part of the human condition and that many of us have moderate amounts of mystical capabilities and some of us are extraordinarily endowed with them. Any culture that ignores and deprecates such capabilities will be successful only so long as the payoffs it produces from its own perspectives are such that the price paid for ignoring the mystical dimensions of our own lives or of the human condition is acceptable. Enlightenment and its offsprings, Science and Technology, were immensely successful in the nineteenth century and up until 1914. But since the Great War, as it was called, the capacity of the Scientific and Enlightenment world views to win assent among even the cultural elites (and the masses were probably never really persuaded) has

112

been declining. The release of atomic energy in 1945, the discovery of the environmental crisis in the middle 1960s, the ethnic, religious, and racial wars that have ravaged the world for the last quarter-century have all shaken the faith many of us shared that salvation would be achieved through the scientific method and technology. Thus we glorified discursive reasoning and excluded all other forms of knowledge. The psychedelic revolution, the mystical revival, the occult culture, the communitarian movement, the hippie life-style, the Woodstock fervor, the counterculture, the emergence of Professor Reich's Consciousness III are all consequences of the failure of the gods of discursive reasoning and positive science. With the characteristic human penchant for swinging from one extreme to the other, we have now produced a group of critics and prophets such as Theodore Roszak and Norman O. Brown who glorify irrationality (or, as they might say, nonrationality) and belittle, when they do not attack, discursive reason. Hyperirrationality or manic nonrationality is the reverse of the old pilgrimage (said to have occurred in both Germany and Texas) from barbarism to decadence without ever pausing at civilization. They move from hypercognitive decadence back to nonrational barbarism without ever seeming to find a middle ground in which it can be asserted that man is both scientist and mystic, thinker and doer, dreamer and practitioner. For brilliant intellectuals like Roszak the complexity of the human condition is too much. If we cannot have the whiteness of one extreme, we will have the blackness of the other; the gray center in which the human race lives is intolerably confused, inelegant, and intellectually unsatisfying.

All of which puts the Christian churches—and Catholicism particularly, I think—in a rather peculiar position. At one time churches had to defend the sacred, the otherworldly, the contemplative against the attack of scientific reason. Now they must defend human reason against the attacks of those who have discovered the sacred and the superstitious once again and who are busily engaged in the process of trying to become pagan mystics. I have the terrible feeling that the lessons of a couple millennia of history may have to be learned all over again.

My guess is that there are two distinct but related cultural phenomena which are absolutely critical in our time and may be the only things remembered about our era a thousand years hence. The first is personalism, the strong and emphatic insistence that man lives not for some otherworldly happiness or for the service of the state, party, or people but for his own personal development, enrichment, and fulfillment. A blend of nineteenth-century liberalism, Marxism, Freudianism, and existentialism, the personalist frame of reference has to a certain extent turned against its progenitors and become so dominant in both the elite and mass cultures that it may be viewed as almost a presupposition. The personalist mystique is part of the very air we breathe. No world view, no symbol system which does not take into account the extraordinary power of personalism will get much of a hearing in contemporary culture. Furthermore, I would think that the personalist thrust is irreversible. Personalism has become part of the dynamic of the human condition, and while it may be modified and developed as the decades of the century go on, it has certainly already become one of the unquestioned criteria by which other ideas, thoughts, and symbols must be evaluated and judged.

The other crucial cultural phenomenon is the one I described in earlier paragraphs: the death of the gods of the Enlightenment and the scientific age. Personalism helped to give the *coup de grâce* to these gods. As long as science and discursive reasoning appeared to be soteriologies that guaranteed human liberation and personal development, a personality-oriented world view could accept them. Once it became clear that science was not in fact freeing man from his chains but making the links stronger and more binding, that man was becoming not more human but less so, the personalists decided that while they were not altogether prepared to dispense with the goods and services that the scientific technostructure make possible (Roszak, after all, does publish books printed by presses and distributed by trucks to be sold in bookstores), they were ready to discuss their assumption of the superiority of discursive reasoning on which the scientific enterprise in fact was built. That one might find another set of philosophical presuppositions to justify science and technology is a proposition that concerns few personalist critics; what concerns most of them is to find a new soteriology, a new model of salvation that will give them hope that man indeed may be liberated from the chains that separate him from his fellow men and the rest of the physical universe.

These two critical cultural developments[1] have obvious implications for man's mystical capabilities, because the mystical experience promises both liberation and fulfillment. We need only read Maslow's strongly personalist account of the peak-experiences of his subjects to perceive the kind of self-fulfillment produced. Similarly, the mystical experience and the world view which it both produces and validates seem to promise a salvation and a liberation that science failed to deliver.

One of the curious aspects of this phenomenon is that it is Oriental mysticism—as manifested in Zen, Yoga, Transcendental Meditation, the teachings of Meher Baba, etc.—that has proven particularly attractive. There are, I think, a number of reasons for this development. The dissatisfaction with the North Atlantic urban industrial civilization is so strong that any world view which legitimates withdrawal from it is bound to be persuasive. Christian mysticism, I fear, would urge not withdrawal but reform, not less commitment but more; and just at this point in time, more commitment is just what America's cultural elites don't want. Furthermore, Eastern mysticism has the perennial attraction of being esoteric and gnostic. It is something strange, unusual, "foreign," and practiced by people who wear turbans or light robes and have mysterious Oriental names. Also there is an element of the secret about Eastern mysticism simply because most people here do not know much about it. The initiate who knows the terms and the techniques, the expectations and the aspirations of the mysterious Orient can persuade himself that he knows something his fellows don't, and hence that he is morally and intellectually superior to them. The strength of the gnostic temptation among America's cultural elite—particularly of the university faculties—should never be minimized.

But probably the most important explanation for the Oriental strain in the current mystical revival is that those institutions re-

[1] I treat them at much greater length in my book *The New Agenda: Towards a Sociological Theology*. New York: Doubleday, 1973.

sponsible for maintaining the Western tradition of mysticism have forgotten all about it. The Catholic Church which produced Augustine, Richard of St. Victor, Catherine of Sienna, Francis of Assisi, John Ruysbroeck, Meister Eckhart, Henry Suso, Richard Rolle, Mechthilde of Magdeburg, Teresa of Avila, and John of the Cross honors these worthies as saints but refuses to take them seriously as teachers or models. Furthermore, those contemporary Catholic ethnics who might have updated the tradition, who might have recorded mystical experiences that are religiously continuous with John of the Cross and Teresa of Avila have not exactly been encouraged to do so. On the contrary, they were warned that getting back into that second-grade classroom or coaching that parish football team was far more important than experiencing or describing ecstasy. On occasion the second-grade classroom and the parish football team were more important than ecstasy, but ecstasy was important, too, and Catholics forgot about it, wrote it off as a phenomenon of the past (if not exactly an aberration of the past) and mentioned it only to the young people with a warning about the dangers involved (and heaven knows there are dangers). Catholics had finally succeeded, in other words, in cutting themselves off completely from their own mystical traditions just at the time when the North Atlantic cultural elites rediscovered with a vengeance the mystical capabilities of the human personality. Roman Catholicism's skill for being in the wrong place at the wrong time has been extraordinarily impressive over the last several centuries.

It is ironic indeed that the church which produced such great mystics of the past and a not insignificant number of ecstatics even in the twentieth century could respond to the modern world's rediscovery of the mystical dimensions of man with nothing more impressive than Catholic Pentecostalism.

There is a good possibility that mysticism will become "trendy." The mass media will discover it for six months and then it will become passé. Just as the rediscovery of mysticism will be big news, so too will its demise. Nothing, of course, will have changed in the world outside. The "revival" will have affected only a few, and its end even less. Like most other social movements of our time, the mystical revival will have no independent existence; it will have been created by the mass media and then executed by it. However, the human capacity for mystical insight will persist. It was not created by best sellers on paperback book racks or by Yoga exercises among fashionable Manhattan neurotics. It will persist long after the trend-setters, the fad creators, and the fashion followers have writen it off as old hat.

Yet some people are deceived by shallow conventional wisdom —particularly young people, who believe everything their college professors say. One year there will be a series of mystical manuals prominently reviewed in *The New York Review of Books* and *The New York Times Book Review,* stories about mysticism in all the fashionable magazines, and maybe a TV special or two. The next year mysticism will be discredited. As I write this book I can see the cycle beginning to move rapidly upward, and by the time this book is in the readers' hands the shallow, superficial, frivolous people who read up on every fad will already be climbing off the mysticism bandwagon. Most "changes" or "trends" one reads about in the newspapers and sees on television are minor revisions of attitudes and behaviors that go on in very small segments of the population that happen to have easy access to the mass media. These people are the ones Dostoyevski had in mind when he said, "They caricaturize everything with which they become associated." They are restless, driven neurotics who fancy themselves a cultural elite and who must, absolutely must, keep up with the latest fashion. But since fashions change quickly, particularly when the nonfashionable catch up, it becomes imperative to move on to something else. Most of the authentic mystics in the country will be untroubled by such phenomenon. They are only dimly aware of the existence of the self-proclaimed cultural elite and cannot imagine that what goes on in their lives has anything in common with Chevy Chase, Cambridge, Berkeley, or the Upper West Side. Neither will serious scholars be upset by watching the ideas developed through the centuries adopted and discarded hastily by a generally uninformed and uncaring group. The rediscovery of mysticism by theologians like Harvey Cox does not revalidate mysticism. Considerable numbers of his fellow Christians have known about it for centuries. Nor will it much matter when at some time in the future he or his imitators decide that mysticism is not relevant, for their decision will not make it less so.

There will come a time when the mystical will become identified with the occult, when all the "important people" will be into it, when having a mystical experience will be "the thing" for all the really sophisticated and "with it" people. There will be a time when mysticism will be an occasion for interpersonal aggression. The fashion-setters are missionaries and proselytizers, and if everyone else is not busy trying to catch up with them, how can they be the avant-garde? Just as there was a time when the self-proclaimed avant-garde was pushing psychoanalysis or political radicalism or nude marathon therapy or astrology, so one can count on being high-pressured by the mystical hard sell in the years ahead. Phony mysticism, fashionable mysticism, "trendy" mysticism, gnostic mysticism is much worse than no mysticism at all.

In the Catholic Church, the search for ecstasy is likely to become the next substitute for faith, restlessly pursued by those pathetic clerics and religious (and some lay people, too) who are desperately looking for solid ground on which to stand. These poor people were raised in the rigid, inflexible post-Tridentine church in which laws, structures, rules, and commands solved every problem. It was not necessary in such a church to face a crisis of faith because the rigid restraints of canonical nonapologetic Catholicism protected one from existential terror on every occasion. But the Vatican Council and the move from the immigrant ghetto to the suburb swept away all of the protective structures, and since the Council these terribly anxious people, desperately searching for some form of certainty, found it for a time in first the Cursillo movement, then in sensitivity training, Pentecostalism, political radicalism, fundamentalism, then in a return to the old devotion (ambiguously termed "nostalgia"), and now in the search for ecstasy. One priest I know was speaking in tongues last year; the year before he presided over sensitivity sessions (with no training, of course); now he spends half an hour each day doing Yoga exercises, which is probably no more irrelevant than the picket lines he used to march in when that was the thing to do. This poor man is afraid to plunge into anything beneath the surface; any kind of experience in depth may force him to face deep questions, questions about his beliefs concerning man's purpose and destiny. He prefers the new gnosis, the new inside story, the new secret that protects him from doubt and terror and convinces him that he is superior to the rest of the ignorant Catholic population which is not agile enough to keep one step ahead of future shock.

Mysticism is no answer to religious doubts, much less a cure for immaturity and shallowness. A mystical interlude can indeed resolve a religious problem, but only occasionally and only for those who can face the problem in all its terrifying ramifications. The post-Conciliar Catholic who has never faced anything in his life with any depth is probably temperamentally incapable now of ever doing so. A mystical interlude and an act of faith are, as we suggested earlier, intimately related, but neither has much to do with the childish self-advertising of the cleric or nun who announces proudly that "I'm not sure what I believe anymore."

Intense psychoanalysis, a thirty-day retreat, a major graduate program in theology, long conferences with a spiritual director or a saint—all of these may be of help to such a person; but standing on his head for a half hour every day hoping that the Holy Spirit will come down to bring him the absolute certainty he had in 1960 can only distract him temporarily from the pain of his own foolishness. One can feel sorry for such a person, but he is not a mystic, and his search for mystical experience is stupid self-delusion.

But will the mystical revival last? Might it not be merely a time-limited phenomenon after all? Might it not be a campus fad that will die as quickly as other fads, the Students for A Democratic Society, for example (remember them)? If we have learned anything in the last decade it is that what today's student generation does is not necessarily the wave of the future. The psychedelic counterculture and the occult revolution may be only passing phenomena. But I am inclined to think that the essence of the renewed interest in mysticism, like its two principal cultural causes—personalism and the death of science—represents an irreversible movement in contemporary cultural history. I think the mystical dimension is part of the structure of the human personality, a part which has been condemned or ignored for a number of centuries. The reasons for minimizing the mystical seem to me to have been eliminated. When we had confidence that a liberal, scientific, optimistic, rational humanism could create a paradise here on earth, there was no particular reason to think it important to try to "break through" to paradise in an interlude of ecstasy. But now that we know that Enlightenment humanism, with all its tools and tricks and skills, cannot build paradise for us, we will begin to explore again that paradise which is both inside and outside of us and which promises yet more to come.

I rather doubt that everybody will become mystics or that mysticism will become the central religious concern of American life as it is, or was, in many of the Eastern lands. But there will be much more interest in mysticism in American culture, and American religions will take on some mystical coloration, which they have lacked previously. Soon it may not be fashionable to be a mystic, and that is just as well; but it will become respectable, perhaps even enviable, and that will put us in an entirely new situation—for our day at least.

# CHAPTER TEN

# Whether To Be a Mystic

I am not the one to write a chapter on how to be a mystic. There are manuals available that detail the exercises required for expanding one's consciousness or for predisposing oneself to mystical knowledge. Buryl Payne's *Getting There Without Drugs* seems to be a sensible description of and commentary on the exercises required for meditation, which presumably prepares the way for ecstasy. If one is interested in the more traditional approach there are the spiritual exercises of St. Loyola, which, incidentally, share some characteristics with the Payne book.

The best I can do is to address myself to the question of whether one should be a mystic. I am scarcely a mystic myself in any ordinary sense of the word; indeed, I am not even very meditative or contemplative. I don't disapprove of either; on the contrary, I respect and admire those qualities. The lack of them in my own personality and character I account as a failing. But for reasons of nature and nurture I am a hard-nosed rational empiricist skeptic. By temperament and training I am one of the least mystical persons I know, and while my preconscious intellect may occasionally take over when I am writing a prose essay, most of my life is marked by strong, vigorous control of the "reality principle," which means that for me deautomatization is virtually impossible. Again, let me insist that I am not saying this is necessarily a good way to be; it is simply the way I am. Anyone coming to my section of the beach looking for a guru might as well pack his things and move to another dune.

In addition, I will confess to having been very skeptical most of my life about mystics, a skepticism that was reinforced by the dreadfully academic mystical theology we were taught in the seminary and by the tremendously dull hagiography we were forced to listen to in what was amusingly called "spiritually reading period." (The principle was that if books weren't read at us, we might never bother to read them ourselves.) It was no accident, then, that I became a nose-counting survey research sociologist, and it was no accident either that my own current research on mysticism involves so much reliance on "hard" data.

But two things have happened to me in the last ten years that have led me to be more sympathetic to the subject of mysticism. First of all, I read some of the poetry of John of the Cross and of Gerard Manley Hopkins. I became conscious that both of these men were articulating the things I believed—but in a far more concrete and far more appealing fashion. Nor was it merely a matter of brilliant poetic insight, though they both had that. John of the Cross and Hopkins clearly had had direct and immediate contact with a reality Out There whose existence I accepted as a matter of abstract intellectual principle; but their descriptions were better than mine, much more appealing, much more impressive, much more seductive. There was, it turned out, something to be said for mystical insight after all.

Then I managed to meet some mystics, or, in a few cases, I discovered that people I already knew were mystics. It turned out that they were not freaks or madmen, prigs, misanthropes, or dull self-righteous clods. On the contrary, they were some of the most interesting and attractive people I had ever met. What was for me a matter of conviction was for them a matter of direct experience (as well as conviction). I then came to believe that religious experience stripped of the creepiness of the language of traditional spirituality and the esoterica of the counterculture might be the crucial element in a contemporary religious situation. God, if He were to be rediscovered at all, would be discovered by most people through some sort of religious experience, an experience which far more people turned out to be capable of than I had ever thought. My position, then, is one of great sympathy for mysticism, but it is a perspective from the outside and restrained somewhat by my feeling that the mystic with an unstable personality (which I suspect is true of most counterculture would-be mystics) is a positive menace to himself and to others.

From this perspective I addressed myself two questions:

1. Can the capacity for mystical ecstasy be developed?
2. If it can, should it be developed?

In response to the first question I would be inclined to say that for many people it cannot be developed, for biological reasons, perhaps, and certainly for psychological reasons. On the other hand, there is evidence in the various research projects underway that a capacity for religious experience is widespread in our society. There are many people, perhaps as much as half the population, who are capable of intense religious experiences. Should this segment of the population assiduously and consciously pursue religious ecstasy?

I will confess to being dubious about the direct pursuit of religious experience, and I am even more dubious about it when it takes place by the injection of chemical substances into the bloodstream. There are three reasons for this skepticism:

1. The goal of human life, according to my religious tradition, is not the pursuit of religious experience but the loving service of others. If ecstasy becomes a goal it is quite likely to become a goal unto itself. Loving service produces far less in the way of emotional

kicks and far more in the way of emotional frustration; it is seldom pursued vigorously.

2. There is very great possibility of self-deception in an ecstatic interlude. One can think one is in direct contact with Reality or that one is receiving a direct message from God when actually all that happens is that one is reading one's own biases, prejudices, preconceptions, and neuroses into an intense emotional experience. Most of the mystics I know are blessedly free from self-deception, but one need only read Norman Cohn and Steven Ozment, as quoted in the last chapter, to see how powerful the temptation to self-deception is.

3. Finally, there should be no doubt that the intense emotional experience of mystical ecstasy can be an immense burden to the personality. Ecstasy and schizophrenia are not the same, yet I know of one person whose experience of what I suspect was an ecstatic interlude pushed him over the edge into a deep schizophrenic episode. I know of another case in which the person admitted to me that he had skirted dangerously close to the edge. Furthermore, "desolation" or "dark night" aspects of ecstasy are only for the bravest and most hardy to endure. No one but a fool would blithely seek experiences which might lead to something like John of the Cross's dark night of the soul. Ecstasy is only for the healthy and mature.

I would conclude that one ought to be extremely skeptical and cautious about the direct pursuit of mystical ecstasy. On the other hand, it also seems to me to be proper to be open to its possibilities. We surely ought not fight our own mystical predispositions if we have them. Nor should we run from them in fear if we feel relatively confident and stable in our "generalized reality-orientation" toward everyday life.

It is entirely appropriate to predispose oneself toward mystical experience by way of various exercises of both traditional spirituality (Eastern or Western) and by contemporary psychological methods of producing partial deautomatization. These exercises seem designed to slow down the perceptual and bodily processes to allow the "rushing in" of mystical experience. Reflection, solitude, withdrawal, contemplation are admirable and perhaps necessary human activities, whether they lead to ecstasy or not. Indeed, they probably do predispose a person for ecstasy only to the extent that he is capable of not being "up tight" about his success in achieving it.

The pursuit of reflection, meditation, and contemplation even to the extent that they may induce quasi-trance states of withdrawal seems to me to be a sensible and healthy activity. Such disciplines should not be confused with psychotherapy; they are not ways to mental health if you haven't got it. To praise reflection and meditation is not a particularly radical position. It will not conflict with what my spiritual advisors in the seminary taught. A guru or a living buddha is not necessary to impart what has a long and valid history in our own culture.

There are all kinds of religious experiences. One does not have to be an ecstatic or believe in the ultimate graciousness of Being or lead a religious life to have such experiences. If one has predisposed oneself toward a religious experience and one comes, well and good; if such experiences don't come, life still goes on, and there is much to understand about it and to do with it.

One of the best descriptions I have seen of a religious experience is contained in the poem "Pentecostal Boogaloo" (written by someone who is anything but a member of the Pentecostal movement in Catholicism):

## POEM FOR PENTECOST

Start with my toes,
you old Ghost
Spirit the soles of my shoes
and teach me a Pentecostal
Boogaloo
Sprain my ankles with dancing
Sandal around my feet,
to roam with me in the rain
and feel at home in my footprints.

Oh! look at me spinning,
Sprinkling, tonguing teaching

Winsoming wondrous steps
lift me, how!?
We'd better quit now,
too all dizzy down giggly
Stop—you're tickling
(my funnybone's fickle for you)
Stop—I'll drop.
I'm dying, I'm flying
with your winding my feet and
legs and waist
Lassoed
Stop chasing fool—I'm racing from you
Don't catch me
Do!
I'll drown!
Oh, drown me—most
For I love you so,
You Old Ghost! [1]

Life is a dance with God's Holy Spirit. I believe that the Holy
Spirit is the principle of variety and playfulness in the universe. It
is the goodness Out There that is skipping around, wheeling and
dealing, cavorting and dancing, calling forth that which is best in
each of us, inviting each of us to that kind of dance that is most
appropriate to our talents, our abilities, and our gifts. The Holy
Spirit is the Goodness outside us, calling to the good inside of us.
As St. Paul puts it: "The Spirit speaks to our spirit." The principle
of variety, playfulness, generosity, and enthusiasm in the universe
speaks to the principle of variety, playfulness, generosity, and enthusiasm that is in each of us and invites each of us to join it. It is
risky, dangerous, breathtaking, exciting, ecstatic, and ultimately, as
the poet suggests, even funny. But the risks and the dangers, the loss
of breath and the humor are different for each one of us. That
which is most noble and generous, most enthusiastic and most committed, most sensitive and loving in me is not the same which is
found in anyone else. I must model my response to the Spirit's in-

[1] Unpublished poem by Nancy G. McCready. Used by permission of the
author.

vitation to the dance on who and what I am and what I hear God's Spirit saying to me.

The medieval theologians were correct. There is a synteresis in us; there is an instinct, an intuition, a capacity for knowing, an ability to "play by ear" which enables us to fit into the variety and playfulness of the universe. That instinct for the Spirit (a dreadfully un-social-scientific term!) must indeed be exercised in community or one ends up as John of Leyden did, a law unto himself. But still no community can substitute for it.

Furthermore—and this is a critical point—our spirit can respond to the Holy Spirit in many different ways. The Spirit does not necessarily communicate in ecstatic rapture; if it does, well and good. It would be disastrous for human life to go out in a desperate quest for rapture, searching for the Holy Spirit and never realizing that that Pentecostal poltergeist is right behind us, waiting for us to turn around to discover what and where he really is. The search for ecstasy that turns off the Spirit where he is in our lives would be tragic and foolish.

God's Spirit is not to be found merely in ecstasy. Much less is he to be found necessarily in the babbling of tongues. He may be present in both places (my guess is that he is present more often in the former; he can speak English if he wants to), but he can be other places too. What is important for each of us is that we find him wherever he is in our own lives.

# CHAPTER ELEVEN

# Mysticism and Christianity

There are three questions I wish to address in this concluding chapter.

First, does the existence of ecstatic experience "prove" the existence of God or the immortality of the human soul?

Second, how is Christian mysticism different from other mysticisms, if indeed it differs at all?

Third, what is the role of ecstatic experience in the Christian life?

All three questions point toward some "practical" conclusions for my explanatory model and my analysis of the meaning of the present mystical revival.

I think the best discussion of mysticism as religious proof may be found toward the end of William James' *The Varieties of Reli-*

*gious Experience.* James concedes that "It [the mystical experience] is on the whole pantheistic and optimistic, or at least the opposite of pessimistic. It is anti-naturalistic, and harmonizes best with twice-borness and so-called other-worldly states of mind." [1] He concludes in effect that there is scientific reason to exclude the possibility that the mystical experience is delusional, but that it may well be a form of systematic self-delusion. Hence James concludes that "non-mystics are under no obligation to acknowledge in mystical states a superior authority conferred on them by their intrinsic nature." [2] But having said that he hedges:

. . . the existence of mystical states absolutely overthrows the pretension of non-mystical states to be the sole and ultimate dictators of what we may believe. As a rule, mystical states merely add a supersensuous meaning to the ordinary outward data of consciousness. They are excitements like the emotions of love or ambition, gifts to our spirit by means of which facts already objectively before us fall into a new expressiveness and make a new connection with our active life. They do not contradict these facts as such, or deny anything that our senses have immediately seized. It is the rationalistic critic rather who plays the part of denier in the controversy, and his denials have no strength, for there never can be a state of facts to which new meaning may not truthfully be added, provided the mind ascend to a more enveloping point of view. It must always remain an open question whether mystical states may not possibly be such superior points of view, windows through which the mind looks out upon a more extensive and inclusive world. [3]

So, according to James, the ecstatic experience may be a monstrous self-delusion, but it may also be an indispensable insight; and he who rejects the insight on a priori grounds is in fact the narrow-minded one. Mystical experience gives us certain hints which may be true and which may even be the most important form of truth.

James states:

Mystical states indeed wield no authority due simply to their being

1 James, *op. cit.*, p. 323.
2 *Ibid.*, p. 326.
3 *Ibid.*, p. 327.

mystical states. But the higher ones among them point in directions to which the religious sentiments even of non-mystical men incline. They tell of the supremacy of the ideal, of vastness, of union, of safety, and of rest. They offer us *hypotheses,* hypotheses which we may voluntarily ignore, but which as thinkers we cannot possibly upset. The supernaturalism and optimism to which they would persuade us may, interpreted in one way or another, be after all the truest of insights into the meaning of this life.[4]

James the thoughtful agnostic says no more than that. Maybe we should believe the intuitions of mysticism and maybe we should not, but at least we should not reject them out of hand. But then James was caught in the boundaries of knowledge and language that the late nineteenth- and early twentieth-century scientific agnosticism imposed on him. Contemporary writers like Jacques Choron and Schubert Ogden, both of whom are dubious about the possibility of human survival, are willing to admit, each in his own way, that the conviction that man survives is built into the structure of human existence. According to Ogden, though, to push that conviction as far as personal survival is selfish; according to Choron, conviction of personal survival could be a form of self-delusion. However, I think that psychological and cultural developments of our time make the agnostic middle ground, which asserts that life does have purpose but brackets the question of human survival with a shrug and a "perhaps," is not nearly as viable an alternative as it used to be. It is much more difficult now to be content with William James' scholarly suspension of judgment in the face of ecstatic experience. Either it tells us something that is extraordinarily hopeful about the universe and about human life, or it is one more cruel joke being played by a Reality that is not only capricious and random but ultimately malign. It grows increasingly necessary to make a choice.

But the choice is not simply one of whether or not mysticism "proves" the existence of God or the immortality of the human soul. The question is both more general and more ultimate, for the real issue is whether Reality is gracious. If it is, it would seem to follow, at least in the personalist world, that man must survive. Built into

4 *Ibid.,* p. 328.

the structure of human existence (and Jacques Choron, the puzzled agnostic, asserts that this is without doubt the case) is a predisposition toward hopefulness. If one turns off the distractions of everyday living but for a moment, one can hear the rumor of Peter Berger's angels. The signals of the transcendent may be wishful thinking, but they are rooted in the core of the human personality, dominating the human unconscious and manifesting themselves in humanity's dreams and symbols and myths the world over. The ecstatic experience is merely one more "rumor of angels," one more signal of the transcendent, one more sign of graciousness; it is the loudest rumor, the most dazzling signal, and the most impressive sign we can expect to have.

The evidence is not such, and in the nature of things can never be such, that an arithmetical formula or a scientific experiment can generate assent. Ultimately one must choose: one must make an act of faith either for graciousness or malignancy and live one's life as though one or the other were true. (And most agnostics I know are cautious, hesitant hopers, at least half expecting a pleasant surprise at the end.)

The fact that some people have ecstatic experiences, even the fact that one has them oneself, does not compel faith. Nevertheless, there is a strain, a predisposition in the ecstatic experience toward hopefulness, indeed toward overwhelming hopefulness, a hopefulness that is latent in the structure of human existence. Whether we choose to be brave enough to accept that hopefulness or cynical enough to dismiss it as wishful thinking is something that each of us must decide for himself. While there are certainly nonreligious ecstasies and apparently some pessimistic ones, almost all of the ecstatic experiences reported in the Western world by the great Christian mystics, by William James, and by Abraham Maslow purport to be encounters with a Reality which was indescribably gracious. Richard Rolle's experience of the "fire of love" may be taken to be paradigmatic of most mystical encounters. Those of us who are not mystics can make of that fact what we will.

In the religions of the East mysticism is the goal and the validation of religious effort. The world in which one lives is unreal; it is composed of transient, ephemeral appearances. By dint of extraordinary self-discipline and control, one is able to eliminate interest in and concern about that world, and then one can open oneself to the Great Reality that absorbs and transforms the self so that all personhood (to use a Western term) is lost. The self becomes lost in the ocean of Being.

It would be a mistake to push this brief and very schematized description of Eastern mysticism too far. Gandhi was not the first of the Indian holy men to be deeply involved in practical political and social affairs. Many Eastern and Western scholars are convinced that the mystical experiences of the Orient and Occident have much more in common than the rhetoric by which they are described would lead us to believe. Still, it seems safe to say that withdrawal and loss of self are ideals in the East in a way that they never have been and probably cannot be in a culture that has been shaped by the Yahwistic (or Judeo-Christian, as I do not like to call it) religious heritage. For the Yahwist believes that the Great Reality is a Thou, a Thou that is a Self, a Self that enters into passionate relationships with humans. Yahweh on Sinai is categorically different from the anthropomorphic gods of the Gentiles, because he transcends his creation definitively and totally. But he is also categorically different from the Ultimate Principle, as described in the Orient, because Yahweh *cares;* he is involved with his people; he carries on a love affair with his creatures. This is neither a superior nor inferior religious notion. Both the Greeks and the Orientals would be horrified by it. The point is that under the illumination provided by such a religious symbol, withdrawal from the world and withdrawal from self are scarcely laudable behaviors. Yahweh is in the world and transcends it. What is more, he is working out his grand design of salvation history in the course of human events. Even in a monastery one views oneself as deeply involved in salvation history.

There can be no I-Thou relationship if one of the partners ceases to be a person. Hence in the Jewish and in particular the Christian mystical tradition it may be said that the self is completely transformed by the Other, yet the self never ceases to exist. The goal is not so much the loss of self in the mystical encounter as it is the transformation of the self for its return to even more vigorous involvement in Yahweh's work in the world. A Gandhi is by way of an exception in the East; in the West he would be the rule. Teresa and John of the Cross reformed the Carmelite order and were deeply involved in Spanish politics; Francis advised popes and emperors; Catherine of Sienna and Bernard both virtually ordered popes to do what they were supposed to do; Eckhart and Rysbroeck were famous preachers; Richard Rolle was a master of spiritual direction. Almost without exception these mystics felt compelled to communicate their experiences to others, and these experiences were their own, not part of some infinite Ocean of Being.

The Christian mystical tradition, then, is one of activist mysticism. Indeed, it is far and away the most activist of all the mystical traditions, perhaps deeply affronting the more quiet contemplative mysticism of the East. Again, I do not want to draw the distinction too sharply. There are activist threads in Eastern mysticism and passive ones in the West, and ultimately both record what are fundamentally similar experiences. But the Christian tradition stands under the shadow of a personal God who demands personal relationships, not the loss of self.[5] What is different about Eastern and Western mysticism is not so much the experience itself as the meaning system which creates the religious context of the experience and whose symbols are used afterwards to describe it. The Christian mystic simply cannot permanently turn off the world; to the extent that he does so, he is false to the world view that is enfleshed in his symbol system.

Hence the mystical experience is not the decisive and distinctive religious activity in the Christian tradition. The Christian is concerned with the coming of the Kingdom of God, with the proclamation of the Good News. There is no possible doubt that the twenty-fifth chapter of St. Matthew—the climax toward which the whole of that gospel is written—enjoins the Christian to loving service, not religious experience and not mystical ecstasy. Jesus watched the separation of the sheep and the goats on a Palestinian hillside as the day came to an end and said that finally the good would be

[5] And of course it is this personal God with his passionate involvement in human life who sets the context for the personalist psychological perspective described in a previous chapter.

separated from the bad because some served the least of the brothers and him and others did not.

Christianity does not condemn mysticism. Contemporary scripture scholars think that both the baptism of Jesus and the Transfiguration were experiences of religious ecstasy. There is a strong mystical strain in the writings attributed to St. John; and St. Paul had something that very much looked like an ecstatic experience at least once. Many, though not all, of the great saints throughout the last two millennia have been occasional if not habitual mystics. The great writings of Christian spirituality surely are ordered toward predisposing Christians for moments of ecstasy. Nonetheless, the ecstasy is secondary to a more effective loving service of the brothers. If ecstasy interferes with such loving service, it is to be viewed with grave suspicion. How the balance between ecstasy and loving service in the lives of the saints was worked out was always a problem for them and for their confused and harassed religious superiors. However, the way the old hagiographers described these problems, the solution was always in the direction of loving service.

So Christianity is far more a this-worldly religion than most of those of the East. As such it is a scandal to many Orientals and to some Westerners who are trying to escape the ugly problems of the contemporary North Atlantic civilization through the withdrawal mysticisms of the East. This is unfortunate, but there is not much we can do about it. However, a kind of ecumenism should be possible by which each of the traditions can approach an understanding of what the other is really saying.

One priest remarked to me recently that he still thought that what we learned in the seminary was true: If you have the gospel and the sacraments, you don't need mysticism, and since it is likely to distract you from your work, it is better to do without it. Surely this is pushing the Christian emphasis on loving service too far. It makes the same mistake as Enlightenment rationalism did in assuming that the mystical dimension of human life was exceptional, even aberrational. I have argued in this book that the capacity for ecstasy is built into the structure of the human personality, and Christianity no more systematically excludes ecstasy than it excludes anything else that is part of the human condition (sin only is excepted, as one of the epistles says). If withdrawal from the world and all its relationships and responsibilities is rejected by the Christian tradition, so is such an involvement in the world that leaves out all possibility of contemplation and reflection. And one really begins to contemplate and reflect when the mystical capacities of the human personality are ready to be actualized. A religion without mysticism would be as un-Christian as one without anything else but mysticism.

Therefore I would think that the Christian churches ought to welcome the mystical revival as forcing them to face once again a forgotten component in their own heritage. We can be properly skeptical about the aberrations of some pseudomystical forms. We can also be cautious and reserved about ecstatic experiences that are held to dispense one from personal and social responsibilities; but we can rejoice when we discover a mystic, because such a person is one of God's own. And we can recognize and encourage the intimations of ecstasy that follow this experience, however transiently, in our daily lives.

That is, we can if we have time to notice them; and this is the whole problem, particularly for those Christians who have made activism completely and totally synonymous with religion and who have thus become incapable of turning the world off for even a moment. It would be absurd to say that the churches must launch active campaigns to produce more mystics; but it would not be absurd at all to say that they should insist more vigorously than they have in the past that solitude and quiet, tranquility and serenity, reflection and contemplation are absolutely indispensable characteristics of the human life. The old spiritual directors in our seminary days repeated these truths, but somehow when they translated them into practice there was never enough time for tuning out distractions and moving toward intimate personal contact with Reality. Probably the reason was that the spiritual directors were all for meditation but skeptical, indeed fearful, of the ecstasy that was sometimes its consequence.

Yet ecstasy is at the core of the Christian tradition. The gospels tell us about two ecstatic experiences of Jesus: the first at the time of his baptism by John, when he saw fully what his vocation was to be; and the second at the moment of Transfiguration, when he saw that it was necessary to go to Jerusalem to die. Scripture scholars tell us that these two stories are part of the most ancient traditions of the early church. It is virtually certain that they recount actual incidents, not stories that the early church produced to explicate its faith. Jesus, indeed, was an ecstatic, and his experience gave direction and purpose to his life and ministry. St. Paul also had ecstatic experiences. On the road to Damascus he experienced a clear ecstasy, and also there was that strange interlude recounted in the twelfth chapter of the epistle to the Corinthians:

But I will move on to the visions and revelations I have had from the Lord. I know a man in Christ who, fourteen years ago, was caught up—whether still in the body or out of the body, I do not know; God knows—right into the third heaven. I do know, however, that this same person—whether in the body or out of the body, I do not know; God knows—was caught up into paradise and heard things which must not and cannot be put into human language. I will boast about a man like that, but not about anything of my own except my weaknesses. If I should decide to boast, I should not be made to look foolish, because I should only be speaking the truth; but I am not going to, in case anyone should begin to think I am better than he can actually see and hear me to be.[6]

But even apart from these episodes St. Paul describes, the epistles are filled with insights which could only have come out of frequent mystical experiences. One can find them almost randomly in his writings. For example, in the eighth chapter of the epistle to the Romans: "Neither death nor life, no prince, nothing that exists, nothing still to come, not any power, or height or depth, nor any created thing, can ever come between us and the love of God made visible in Christ Jesus our Lord" (Romans 8:38–39). Similarly, the Johannine works are shot through with the language of divinity and love and mystical insight. The man who wrote the prologue to the fourth gospel was clearly one whose ecstatic visions commanded and directed his thought.

In addition to the Christian mystics quoted in earlier chapters,

[6] Corinthians II, 12:2–6. The Jerusalem Bible.

such leaders of decisive change in Christianity as Francis of Assisi, Martin Luther, and Ignatius of Loyola obviously had frequent ecstatic experiences. If ecstasy is not the absolutely essential dimension of Christianity, it has been often the driving force in the development of the Christian tradition. There have been madmen as well as saints in that tradition, and in some cases it was hard for their contemporaries to tell the difference. The Christian practice has been to judge revelations deriving from ecstatic experience by the context in which the revelation occurred. And it was often difficult to evaluate the context. Not every person who claims to have seen a mystic vision, nor every person who has in fact seen a mystic vision, can lay claim to being an authentic interpreter of the Christian tradition and expect to be accepted by the Christian community. In both its official and its unofficial, informal structures, Christianity seems to have combined an open mind with polite skepticism about its mystics. It has been ready to be persuaded, but never to be easily persuaded. Mystical ecstasy is an integral part of Christianity. The Christian knows, however, that the universe is animated by love without having to have immediate and direct experience of that love. He is committed to living a life that reflects such love. If he experiences the love that binds the universe together, so much the better. Such an experience will fuel the flames of his own commitment to loving service. He does not reject mystical ecstasy; he does not expect it; he is grateful for it. If he seeks it out he does not do it in such a way as to interfere with his loving service to others.

The Christian can scarcely deny the existence of a Reality which is outside the boundaries of ordinary time and ordinary space. On the contrary, he is firmly committed to the conviction that the extraspatial and extratemporal Reality has manifested itself repeatedly in the human condition, most especially in the life and death and resurrection of Jesus Christ. Reality, then, is not just appearance, not just randomness, not just chance, not just absurd capriciousness. The Christian who is convinced of this must concede that Reality has the right to disclose itself in any way it chooses. He must also concede that this "other dimension" of Reality can be perceived in different ways by different people. Mystical ecstasy is just one way— according to those who have experienced it, it is the supreme way—

of encountering that other dimension. But for the Christian it cannot be the only way of religious experience. Yet given these presuppositions there is no reason to contest the claim of those who have had ecstatic interludes that theirs is the religious experience par excellence.

It is not just in religious mysticism or sexual union or murky drug trips that man breaks out of the boundaries of ordinary time and space. The height of a mountain, the expanse of an ocean or a lake, a fresh breeze at the end of a hot summer day, a child struggling to walk across the lawn, a flash of lightning, the elaborate design of a Picasso painting, the feel of a sailboat dancing over the waters, the sight of a human body—male or female—on the beach may all force us out of the limitations of our selfhood and the dull, monotonous, gray-tinged life of ordinary space and daily duration. These are moments of intimation of ecstasy, potential triggers, predisposing experiences which, if we pause but a moment longer to appreciate them, could push us to the edge of a form of knowledge of which we are all capable. The Spirit of God is out there, whirling and swirling, wheeling and dealing, and he is also inside of us, enveloping us with fire and warmth and what Richard Rolle called "great and unexpected comfort."

The fire is there if we but give it spark.

# Varieties and Descriptions of Religious Experiences

Appendix A represents the questions asked in our national survey, along with the responses in percentages. (N = 1467.)

### MYSTICAL AND PSYCHIC EXPERIENCES IN A NATIONAL SAMPLE OF AMERICANS
*(Percent)*

| WITH WHAT FREQUENCY HAVE YOU HAD ANY OF THE FOLLOWING EXPERIENCES? | NEVER IN MY LIFE | ONCE OR TWICE | SEVERAL TIMES | OFTEN | I CANNOT ANSWER THIS QUESTION |
|---|---|---|---|---|---|
| A. Thought you were somewhere you had been before, but knowing that it was impossible. | 38 | 29 | 24 | 6 | 3 |

## MYSTICAL AND PSYCHIC EXPERIENCES (cont.)

| WITH WHAT FREQUENCY HAVE YOU HAD ANY OF THE FOLLOWING EXPERIENCES? | NEVER IN MY LIFE | ONCE OR TWICE | SEVERAL TIMES | OFTEN | I CANNOT ANSWER THIS QUESTION |
|---|---|---|---|---|---|
| B. Felt as though you were in touch with someone when they were far away from you. | 40 | 26 | 24 | 8 | 2 |
| C. Seen events that happened at a great distance as they were happening. | 72 | 14 | 8 | 2 | 4 |
| D. Felt as though you were really in touch with someone who had died. | 70 | 16 | 8 | 3 | 2 |
| E. Felt as though you were very close to a powerful, spiritual force that seemed to lift you out of yourself. | 61 | 18 | 12 | 5 | 3 |

Ask the following questions only of those who answer "E" "once or twice," "several times," or "often": Many people who have had such experiences say that there are "triggers" or specific events that set them off. Have any of the following events ever started such an experience for you?

## "DESCRIPTORS" OF MYSTICAL EXPERIENCE

| DESCRIPTORS | PERCENT |
|---|---|
| A feeling of deep and profound peace | 55 |
| A certainty that all things would work out for the good | 48 |
| Sense of my own need to contribute to others | 43 |
| A conviction that love is at the center of everything | 43 |
| Sense of joy and laughter | 43 |
| An experience of great emotional intensity | 38 |
| A great increase in my understanding and knowledge | 32 |
| A sense of the unity of everything and my own part in it | 29 |
| A sense of a new life or living in a new world | 27 |
| A confidence in my own personal survival | 27 |
| A feeling that I couldn't possibly describe what was happening to me | 26 |

| | |
|---|---:|
| The sense that all the universe is alive | 25 |
| The sensation that my personality has been taken over by something much more powerful than I am | 24 |
| A sense of tremendous personal expansion, either psychological or physical | 22 |
| A sensation of warmth or fire | 22 |
| A sense of being alone | 19 |
| A loss of concern about worldly problems | 19 |
| A sense that I was being bathed in light | 14 |
| A feeling of desolation | 8 |
| Something else | 4 |

Approximately how long did your experience(s) (average time if more than one) last?

## TRIGGERS OF MYSTICAL EXPERIENCES

| TRIGGERS | PERCENT |
|---|---:|
| Listening to music | 49 |
| Prayer | 48 |
| Beauties of nature such as sunset | 45 |
| Moments of quiet reflection | 42 |
| Attending church service | 41 |
| Listening to sermon | 40 |
| Watching little children | 34 |
| Reading the Bible | 31 |
| Being alone in church | 30 |
| Reading a poem or a novel | 21 |
| Childbirth | 20 |
| Sexual lovemaking | 18 |
| Your own creative work | 17 |
| Looking at a painting | 15 |
| Something else | 13 |
| Physical exercise | 1 |
| Drugs | 0 |

Those who have had religious experiences have given various descriptions of what they were like. Here is a list of some of the things they say happen. Have any of them happened to you during any of your experiences?

### DURATION OF MYSTICAL EXPERIENCE

| DURATION | PERCENT |
| --- | --- |
| A few minutes or less | 37 |
| Ten or fifteen minutes | 13 |
| Half an hour | 6 |
| An hour | 5 |
| Several hours | 9 |
| A day or more | 21 |
| No answer | 8 |

# Varieties of
# Altered States
# of Consciousness*

## *A. REDUCTION OF EXTEROCEPTIVE STIMULATION AND/OR MOTOR ACTIVITY*

In this category are included mental states resulting primarily from an absolute reduction of sensory input, from a change in patterning of sensory data, or from constant exposure to repetitive, monotonous stimulation. A drastic reduction of motor activity also may prove an important contributing factor.

1. Highway or road hypnosis
2. "Breakoff" phenomena in high-altitude jet pilots
3. Mental aberrations while at sea, in the Arctic, or on the desert
4. Experimental sensory-deprivation states

\* From Arnold Ludwig, "Altered States of Consciousness," in Raymond Prince (ed.), *Trance and Possession States*. Montreal: R. M. Bucke Memorial Society, 1968.

5. Alterations in consciousness associated with solitary confinement or prolonged social isolation, such as commonly practiced by ascetics or mystics
6. Post-cataract operation psychoses
7. Nocturnal hallucinations, especially in elderly persons
8. Mental aberrations in elderly cataract patients
9. Extreme boredom
10. Alterations in consciousness in poliomyelitis patients placed in a tank-type respirator
11. Mental aberrations in polyneuritis patients with sensory anesthesias and motor paralysis
12. Mental phenomena experienced during profound immobilization in a body cast or traction
13. Hypnagogic and hypnopompic states
14. Sleep and associated phenomena, such as dreaming, somnambulism
15. Healing and revelatory states during "incubation" or "temple sleep," as practiced by the early Egyptians, Greeks, and Romans
16. "Kayak disease," found in Greenlanders spending several days in a kayak while hunting seals
17. Hypnotic trance

## B. INCREASE OF EXTEROCEPTIVE STIMULATION AND/OR MOTOR ACTIVITY AND/OR EMOTION

In this category are included excitatory mental states resulting primarily from sensory overload or bombardment, which may or may not be accompanied by strenuous physical activity or exertion. Profound emotional arousal and mental fatigue may also be major contributing factors.

1. Suggestible mental states produced by "third degree" tactics, such as grilling and verbal badgering
2. Brainwashing states
3. Experimental "hyperalert" or "hyperkinetic" trance states secondary to tension-induction maneuvers
4. Dance- and music-trance in response to jazz, rock'n'roll, rhythmic drumming
5. Hyperkinetic trance states associated with emotional contagion, often encountered in a group or mob setting such as manifested by mass hysteria or the St. Vitus and tarantism dancing epidemics of the Middle Ages
6. Religious conversion and healing-trance experiences during revivalistic meetings
7. Mental aberrations associated with certain rites of passage (e.g., puberty and initiation rites), such as found in initiates to manhood status in some primitive tribes or the Greater Eleusinian Mysteries

8. "Spirit possession" states, either by the Holy Spirit or tribal spirits, during revivalistic or tribal religious ceremonies

9. Shamanistic, divination, and prophetic trance states during certain tribal ceremonies

10. Ecstatic trance, such as experienced by the "howling" or "whirling" dervishes during their famous *devr* dance

11. Trance-like states experienced during prolonged masturbation

12. Orgiastic trance, such as experienced by the Bacchanalians or Satanists during certain religious rites

13. Fire walker's trance

14. Alterations in consciousness arising primarily from inner emotional turbulence or conflict, or secondary to external conditions conducive to heightened emotional arousal
    *a*) fugue states, amnesias, traumatic neuroses
    *b*) battle fatigue
    *c*) panic states, rage reactions
    *d*) increased suggestibility, illusions, etc., resulting from prolonged fear
    *e*) depersonalization
    *f*) hysterical conversion reactions, dreamy and dissociative states
    *g*) berserk, latah, and whitico psychoses
    *h*) bewitchment and demoniacal possession states
    *i*) acute psychotic states, such as schizophrenic reactions

## C. DECREASED ALERTNESS OR RELAXATION OF CRITICAL FACULTIES

Grouped within this category are mental states which appear to occur mainly as a result of what might best be described as a "passive state of mind," in which active, goal-directed thinking is minimal.

1. Mystical, transcendental or revelatory states (e.g., *satori, samādhi*, nirvana, cosmic consciousness, at-oneness with nature) attained through passive meditation or occurring spontaneously during the relaxation of one's critical faculties

2. Daydreaming

3. Drowsiness

4. Brown study, or reverie

5. Free-associative states during psychoanalytic therapy

6. Mediumistic trance

7. Deliberately induced autohypnotic trance (e.g., among Indian fakirs, mystics, Pythian priestesses, etc.)

8. Creative, illuminatory, and insightful states

9. Profound aesthetic experiences

10. Music-trance, especially common while absorbed in relaxing, soothing lullabies
11. Reading-trance, especially with poetry
12. Alterations in consciousness associated with profound cognitive and muscular relaxation, such as during floating on the water, sunbathing
13. Nostalgia

## D. PRESENCE OF SOMATOPSYCHOLOGICAL FACTORS

Included under this heading are mental states resulting primarily from alterations in body chemistry or neurophysiology. These alterations may be deliberately induced or may result from conditions over which the individual has little or no control.

1. Hypoglycemia, either spontaneous or secondary to fasting; ascetics or priests may fast as an aid in inducing mystical or spirit-possession states
2. Drowsiness secondary to hyperglycemia (e.g., postprandial lethargy)
3. Dehydration (often partially responsible for the mental aberrations encountered on the desert or at sea)
4. Hormonal disturbances, especially of the thyroid, adrenal medulla and cortex, may produce psychotic states
5. Narcolepsy
6. Auras preceding migraine or epileptic seizures
7. Hyperventilation states
8. Alterations in consciousness subsequent to sleep deprivation
9. Toxic delirious states secondary to the abrupt withdrawal from addicting drugs, such as barbiturates, alcohol, etc.
10. Toxic deliria caused by fever or the ingestion of toxic agents
11. Dreamy states and *déjà vu* phenomena caused by temporal-lobe seizures
12. The administration of pharmacological agents
    a) anesthetics: e.g., $CO_2$, $NO_2$, ether
    b) LSD and related compounds
    c) narcotics, marihuana
    d) sedatives: e.g., barbiturates, alcohol
    e) stimulants: e.g., amphetamine, cocaine
    f) others: e.g., Sernyl, Ditran, etc.

# Index